T0129694

He Was There All the Time

NICK HOFFMAN

WESTBOW
PRESS®
A DIVISION OF THOMAS NELSON
& ZONDERVAN

This book is a work of non-fiction. Unless otherwise noted, the author and the publisher make no explicit guarantees as to the accuracy of the information contained in this book and in some cases, names of people and places have been altered to protect their privacy.

WestBow Press books may be ordered through booksellers or by contacting:

WestBow Press
A Division of Thomas Nelson & Zondervan
1663 Liberty Drive
Bloomington, IN 47403
www.westbowpress.com
1 (866) 928-1240

Because of the dynamic nature of the Internet, any web addresses or links contained in this book may have changed since publication and may no longer be valid. The views expressed in this work are solely those of the author and do not necessarily reflect the views of the publisher, and the publisher hereby disclaims any responsibility for them.

Scripture taken from the New King James Version®. Copyright © 1982 by Thomas Nelson. Used by permission. All rights reserved.

ISBN: 978-1-9736-8831-0 (sc)
ISBN: 978-1-9736-8830-3 (hc)
ISBN: 978-1-9736-8832-7 (e)

Library of Congress Control Number: 2020904661

Print information available on the last page.

WestBow Press rev. date: 4/1/2020

Contents

Acknowledgement

This book took about six months to assemble. It has taken a lifetime to write.

In recognizing the cast that has made it all possible, I humbly and lovingly acknowledge the unmerited favor of God, my Heavenly father, whose "grace hath brought me safe thus far, and grace will lead me home."

My life could never have been as rich and rewarding without the love, inspiration and encouragement of Nan, my beloved grandmother, Josephine Hoffman; and her son and my father, Kenneth D. Hoffman. They have been and always will be the wind beneath my wings.

In addition to his many contributions, Dad collaborated closely with me in the arrangement of the book and painstakingly edited several proofs of it from Omaha, Neb.

I have been immeasurably blessed by the family (photos of them sprinkled throughout the book) and friends I have written about, in addition to many, many others to whom my admiration, though unwritten, is no less heartfelt. Their love, friendship, prayers and encouragement have blessed with me a life I never could have imagined and whose richness is far more than I deserve.

I am grateful to the newspaper I called home for 30 years, the Courier-Express/Tri-County Sunday, for affording me a platform in which to share my thoughts and experiences. Some of the columns were printed while the newspaper was owned and published by McLean Publishing, DuBois, PA between Jan. 1, 1988, and March 31, 2013, and are reproduced with permission. Others appeared in the newspaper by current owner and publisher Tioga Publishing, Wellsboro, PA, since March 31, 2013; they are also reprinted with permission. In addition to acknowledging the professionalism and support of the staffs I worked with, I cheerfully thank publishers Jason Gray Jr., W. Dock Lias, Denny Bonavita and Pat Patterson.

Finally, the talented professionals at WestBow Press led and encouraged me through every step of the process of publishing my first (but hopefully not my last) book: Kris Jeffries, Jill Zane, Brady Adams, Juvy Luzon, Nolan Estes, Tim Finch, Bob De Groff and Teri Watkins.

Preface

Who are we, that He is mindful of us?

That is an intriguing question.

Have you ever looked up into the sky on a starry night and tried to comprehend where – or even if – you fit in the overall scheme of a vast universe? Within that universe are billions of galaxies. One of those galaxies is the Milky Way. It includes Earth, its solar system, the sun and billions of stars.

Earth has seven continents, 195 countries, 197 million square miles and about 7 1/2 billion people.

If that is too much to digest in one bite, try this either/or question: **Either** everything described above is the result of a random "Big Bang" billions of years ago after which some cellular goo evolved into man (and all the other critters that inhabit land, seas and sky), **or** it is the product of a very deliberate plan by God the Creator, the Alpha and Omega, the beginning and the end. Take your time – it's an open book test that lasts a lifetime.

Let's focus on a single one of those 7 1/2 billion people. The human body is made up of trillions of cells within a framework of nerves, tissues, organs, muscle, ligaments, tendons and bones that are maintained and sustained by circulatory, digestive, endocrine, immune, integumentary, lymphatic, musculoskeletal, nervous, reproductive, respiratory and urinary systems.

Two of those organs, the heart and the brain, play outsize roles in keeping everything going.

The heart is the "pump" that supplies the blood that provides oxygen and nutrients to all parts of the body so they can function, while also taking away waste that must be disposed of before it builds to toxic levels. Over a normal lifetime, it is estimated that the heart will beat more than 3 billion times and pump about 1 million barrels of blood. It beats on its own - every second, every minute, every hour, every day, every year.

The brain, which is also nourished by the blood the heart is busy pumping, takes care of thought, emotion, memory and the senses, primarily vision, hearing, taste and smell.

The scientific community relies on provably true facts gleaned from experiments and empirical research. It chooses option "goo" to explain everything that ever has been, is or will be, since God can't be reduced to an integer in a calculation on a blackboard.

I'm a King David man. I envision him lying on the ground on a warm summer night in 1000 B.C., looking up into that starry night sky when he wrote Psalm 8:3-4 - "When I consider Your heavens, the work of Your fingers, the moon and the stars, which You have set in place, what is man that You are mindful of him, ..."

During Creation, God saved His best – You and me - for last. That is why He is mindful of us. We've come a long way since that "D'oh!" moment in the Garden of Eden. Scientists can explain some of it, but not all.

We do not walk alone. We have company. More than we know.

Prologue

Some of the columns that are interspersed throughout this book make reference to the area of west-central Pennsylvania where I've lived all my life.

My hometown of Brockway is in Jefferson County which, along with Elk and Clearfield counties, forms what is widely known in these parts as the Tri-County Area.

The area's population was 172,630 in 1900. After it ballooned to 200,361 in 1920, it has been in a slow, steady decline ever since, to an estimated 153,198 in 2018.

When my great-grandfather arrived at Ellis Island from "the Old Country" in 1900 at the age of 7, Brockway's population was 1,777. It peaked at 2,709 shortly after my Dad's birth in 1938. The latest estimate is 2,046.

The regional commerce, retail and finance center is DuBois which, together with Sandy Township that surrounds it, is also the largest population center in the Tri-County. "Greater DuBois" had a population of 12,597 in 1900, peaked at 20,508 in 1920 and was 17,830 in 2018.

When I was a youngster, shoppers spent the day in downtown DuBois in the days before the DuBois Mall was built in the early 1970s. All the stores were there: Montgomery Ward's and J.C. Penney, Sears, Turner's and Newberry's, along with two theaters, restaurants and a daily newspaper among other attractions.

I made my living at that daily newspaper, the Courier-Express, for 30 years, from the time I joined the staff as a sportswriter in 1984 until I left in 2014 after 13 years as managing editor.

For generations dating into the early and mid-1800s, the local economy has risen and fallen with the fortunes of resource-based and manufacturing enterprises: lumber, coal, railroads, glass containers, clay and powdered metals.

The healthcare industry is taking an increasingly pre-eminent role in the current economy and DuBois will soon be a regional destination for that service, too.

Farms still dot the landscape. So do rivers and streams and forests, where hunting, fishing and outdoor recreation are not only good for us but for our economy, too.

Pittsburgh, Buffalo and Cleveland are within a 3-hour drive. Chicago and New York City are about 8 hours away. We like to think we're close enough to "civilization" but also far enough away from it.

The major thoroughfares that connect us to those far-enough-away places are Interstate 80, which runs east-west, and U.S. Route 219, which snakes its way north-south.

We sit near the confluence of the western and north central Allegheny Plateaus in the Allegheny Mountains, near the, what else? - Allegheny National Forest and Allegheny River.

There are plenty of Churches ... : Catholic, Presbyterian, Methodist, Free Methodist, Lutheran, Episcopal, Christian & Missionary Alliance, Jehovah Witness, Church of Jesus Christ of Latter Day Saints, Orthodox, Jewish, Nazarene and a host of unaffiliated congregations.

... and plenty of clubs: Moose, Elks, Eagles, Lions, various incarnations of Sportsmans, Sportsmen's or Sportsman's, VFW, American Legion, Oddfellows, Pulaski, Sons and Daughters of Italy, Rotary, Kiwanis,

Kaimanns, Army-Navy, Jaycees and Independent Political & Social among them.

We have each other's backs and pitch in to "bear one another's burdens." Fire protection throughout the three counties is all-volunteer.

My "stomping grounds" included such exotic locations as Munderf, Richardsville and Hazen, which are along or near Route 28 between Brockway and Brookville, the county seat to the southwest. To the north, along or not far from Route 219 are Crenshaw, Brockport, Kersey, Brandy Camp, Shawmut, Boot Jack Summit and Ridgway, the Elk County seat. Oops; almost forgot Dagucahonda and Dagus Mines.

Like many places in rural America, this is a nice place to call home, even though fewer and fewer are doing so with each passing generation.

Last but not least, we have our idiosyncrasies:

* There are a lot of "creeks" in the area, pronounced "cricks."
* On a hot summer day, we drink "pop" instead of "soda."
* When referring to a small group of family, friends, enemies or strangers, we use the collective "you'ns" or "you-uns."
* Finally, we freely confess – and make no apology for - clinging to our guns and our Bibles.

Cast of Characters

While you are getting acclimated with the "flow" of this book, it may help to list of some of the characters who are referred to early on but not fully identified until later:

* Nan and Papa – Ken & Josephine Hoffman, my paternal grandparents.
* Wee Wee and Auntie Rose – William Repiscak, my paternal grandmother's brother, and his wife.
* Bubba – John F. Repiscak, my great-grandfather.
* Redford "Pa" Segers – pioneer lumberman, my great-great-great-grandfather.
* Frone & Mabel Segers – Pa Segers' daughters to his second wife.

Introduction

We humans have an instinctual need to "belong" and be part of something. It is one of the pillars upon which civilizations are built.

Our need for each other has been expressed since people came together for their mutual benefit – food, shelter, security and, to keep the ball rolling, mating.

How much time we spend interacting with each other is a matter of choice. I prefer solitude, but I've spent a fair amount of time in the middle of people, and don't mind that either.

It is particularly impossible to avoid people when you're in the newspaper business, as I was. Even in a small town, people get to know you and you get to know them.

The newspaper gave me a platform from which to share my thoughts with readers, often in a column. Many of them were inspired when someone who'd impacted my life passed away. It happened so frequently that Editor/Publisher Denny Bonavita's standard reply when I told him, "I have a column for you to look at" was, "Who died?"

I thought about compiling those columns into a volume of "reflections" on growing up in Brockway, something that might be of interest to the families and friends of those I wrote about.

Periodically over the last 20 years, the idea flickered,

then faded but was never completely extinguished. It went onto a "one of these days" lists we all make. I just never seemed to have the time.

During my annual trip to Nebraska in 2019 to visit my Dad, I came down with a respiratory infection that kept me inside and under the weather for most of the two weeks I was there. Vacation ruined, right? Wrong. This was the time I never seemed to be able to find to get started. Inspiration struck and I realized I had an opportunity to do more than a reminiscences book. I put pen to paper and started writing.

I begin with the premise that each of us is in part a product of the influence of others upon us: Family, friends, teachers, preachers, doctors, lawyers, Indian chiefs, butchers, bakers and candlestick makers.

Each of us has a favorite teacher, or a best friend (BFF in today's parlance), or someone who had a lasting impact on our life. Name yours.

Wherever we are in our journey through life, we haven't gotten there by ourselves. With the spread of the Internet and social media, it is virtually impossible to completely isolate ourselves, no matter how tempting it may be at times to do so.

Clarence Oddbody, the Guardian Angel in "It's a Wonderful Life," said it this way near the climax of that 1946 movie starring James Stewart: "Strange, isn't it? Each man's life touches so many other lives. When he isn't around he leaves an awful hole, doesn't he?"

That is, hands down, my all-time, no-doubt-about-it favorite movie. Since the first time I watched it in 1984 and cried as Harry Bailey proposed a toast "To my big brother George" - I've thought about how each of us at some point in our lives is cast as a George (or Georgette) Bailey.

We have our hands full every day navigating the world around us, the one we see, the one we live in. Beyond that, there is an unseen world made up of a dizzying array – billions and billions - of individual paths crisscrossing and intersecting with incomprehensible frequency and intensity.

Picture an enormous cosmic pinball machine, with all those little silver balls bouncing into and off each other and being redirected with every impact. That's how I envision it.

It is in that realm that I believe an omnipotent God orders our lives so that each of us is afforded an opportunity to know Him better, to be embraced in His boundless love and be His eyes and ears, hands and feet in the world.

I do not believe "ordering" means the outcomes of each situation are a foregone conclusion. We are created in His image; we are not robots or puppets. We have minds of our own – free will - and can chart our own courses, make wrong choices and pursue our own destinies.

For a long time, I failed to appreciate the interconnectedness of life.

Whoever said, "Life is a journey, not a destination," was right. Life is rarely a straight line from here to there. The people we encounter on our journey are on journeys of their own and all of us are navigating our way through that Great Pinball Machine and its flippers, buzzers and bells.

If we can entertain the concept and imagine how that would look, we can begin to fashion answers to weighty questions like, "What am I doing here?"

Near the end of the movie "Inherit the Wind," the agnostic lawyer played by Spencer Tracy laments the sudden death of his courtroom adversary, an evangelical minister played by Fredric March. Swept up in the passion and glamour of a sensational trial, March's character "got lost and looked for God too far up and too far away." How often are we guilty of doing the same thing?

Each of us is surrounded by a supporting cast that accompanies us from the cradle to the grave. Some are there every step of the way, others for just a fleeting moment. And while we're being enriched by our supporting cast, we are members of other peoples' supporting casts, impacting them. Most of the time, we're not aware of it and often chalk it up to "coincidence."

The story that is going to unfold consists of autobiographical information woven together with columns I wrote about some of the people who made a difference in my life. The columns are distinguished by being in *italics.*

The names and circumstances will differ, but you may recognize from your own experiences some of the events that are described or the characters who are introduced. When you do, smile and appreciate that even with the trials, tears, toils and torments each of us endures from time to time, this is a wonderful life indeed.

A Night to Remember

A lot of people have been involved in my life, not least of them my Dad, Kenneth D. Hoffman.

He made two decisions that profoundly impacted me. The first was to marry and mate with my mother. The second was to divorce her.

While many American families were tuned in to "Lassie," "The Ed Sullivan Show" or "Bonanza" on the evening of Sunday, Oct. 22, 1961, Dad and Mom were welcoming me into the world at DuBois Hospital. I tipped the scales at 8 pounds, 10 ounces.

Dr. Nicholas Lorenzo delivered me and was the first person to leave his mark on me – a scar on my left cheek from his forceps.

He is also the source of my second middle name, preceded by Kenneth - after Dad - and Albert, my mother's father, followed by the family surname.

Kenneth Albert Nicholas Hoffman; Nick, for short.

Dad and I share the same first name as his father. Since we all lived in the same house, there had to be a way to distinguish us. My Grandmother called her husband Papa and her son "Duane," his middle name. My ears perked up and I wagged my tail when someone called "Nick!" So much for a Kenneth Conundrum.

That second big decision occurred in 1972. Since

they were married on Friday the 13th in February 1959 and had been married for 13 years when they split up, those suffering from Triskaidekaphobia would say it was a numbers thing.

The actual reasons were more substantive but in any event, it was a life-altering decision for all of us.

I didn't and couldn't understand it then, but years later I began to appreciate an "unseen hand" and an intricate chain of events that not only changed Dad's life but ended up saving mine.

Forty years after that night in the kitchen, I shared that realization in a column in late summer 2012.

It was an August night in 1972, the 10th I think. I was two months shy of my 11th birthday as the family gathered in the kitchen of our home.

Dad was there to say good-bye. He and Mom were getting divorced and he was leaving.

Where are you going? He didn't know.

Can I go with you? No, son, you can't.

So many questions; so few answers.

He got a ride to the Ohio border, went to Michigan and eventually hitched a ride from a man named Paul Hoover. His trail stopped in Denver, Colo. At age 34, Dad was starting from scratch.

He got a job at a tire factory, worked selling insurance and labored at a steel foundry and a convenience store before he finally latched onto a job with United Parcel Service, where he worked for a quarter century and rose into the regional echelon of corporate communications before he retired.

He's made his share of return trips to Pennsylvania, including sojourns to bury his grandfather and his father and mother. I've spent a couple weeks with him nearly every summer but I haven't spent more than a month of any calendar year with my Dad in 40 years.

I know, though, that no father and son are closer than we are.

We enriched the shareholders of AT&T with our marathon phone conversations and did our part to keep the U.S. Postal Service in business.

This year will be extra special because it marks the 20th anniversary of my stint in Norton, Kan., at Valley Hope drug addiction and alcohol rehabilitation center. Dad and I have only missed a return trip to Norton once since our first visit in 1992.

If Paul Hoover hadn't picked Dad up he wouldn't have ended up in Denver. If he hadn't ended up in Denver, he wouldn't have gone to work for UPS. If he hadn't gone to work for UPS, he wouldn't have moved to Omaha. And if he hadn't moved to Omaha . . . that's the rest of the story.

I was arrested for DUI - my second offense - in February 1992. My blood alcohol was a lofty 0.278 percent, about 3 1/2 times today's legal limit. Every facet of my life was out of control and the trajectory of decline was accelerating. I lived to drink; everything else was secondary.

Luckily, I was eligible for treatment rather than a 30-day stay in the Jefferson County jail. I asked Dad to find out what treatment centers were located in Omaha. I wanted him, if at all possible, to be part of my last stab to turn my life around.

He called a hotline number. I don't know how many people staffed the line that day or how many lines were ringing when Dad called but the lady who answered told him what was available. And then she told him something more.

Her son served in the military in Europe. He came home

with drug and alcohol problems. He went to a place called *Valley Hope* in *Norton, Kan.*, she said, and it saved his life. Dad contacted *Valley Hope*, which is one of the top 10 treatment centers in the U.S. I gave the information to the probation officers and District Attorney's staff and, with their blessing and that of DuBois psychologist Bill Allenbaugh and Judge William Henry, I was on my way to Kansas.

If Dad hadn't called that day at exactly the time when he did; if anyone but her had answered; if we never heard of *Valley Hope* . . . But he did and she did and we did.

On Monday, Sept. 21, 1992, after I checked in, Dad and I went to the chapel at *Valley Hope*, knelt, wept and begged God for a miracle. He said yes. Today, through the grace of God, I am sober and have been for nearly 20 years. (27 and counting as this book is written.)

I'm so looking forward to this year's trip. The plane ticket's bought and paid for. *Valley Hope* knows I'm coming and I'll be making a reservation at the Brooks Motel at the corner of routes 36 and 183, where we've spent a few nights, including Sept. 6, 1995, watching Baltimore's Cal Ripken Jr. eclipse Lou Gehrig's record of consecutive baseball games played.

Ironically, this year includes a trip to Denver, after our stop in Norton, to play golf with some of our buddies from Omaha.

Dad started over when he was 34; I was 31 when my turn came. Both involved a trip "out West," one that we'll share in its entirety this year.

Who could imagine, let alone fathom, that the darkest days of our lives would be stitched together so meticulously, so miraculously?

Rod Stewart recorded the song "Faith of the Heart" as the title song of the 1998 movie, "Patch Adams," starring Robin Williams. Some of the lyrics go like this:

Nick Hoffman

I know the wind's so cold,
I've seen the darkest days.
But now the winds I feel,
Are only winds of change.
I've been through the fire,
And I've been through the rain,
But I'll be fine.

That tune will echo in my head as Dad and I head west this year ... together.

Country Roads, Take Me Home

I didn't know it at the time, but that night in the kitchen was the end of my youthful innocence and marked the start of a long and winding road that continues as I near the end of my sixth decade.

As kids, we're so much in awe of how big the world around us seems that we aren't preoccupied by how seemingly small and inconsequential we are. That perspective affords the fertile field on which we chase aspirations like they were butterflies.

I spent a lot of time at my great-grandfather's house on Arch Street on the outskirts of Brockway. It was soooo big … the main house, grandpa's garden, a garage, the "Little House" outbuilding, giant weeping willows, a goldfish pond and a horse barn.

In the middle of it all was a big apple tree, next to the well. A swing was anchored to a thick bough and provided a throne from where I could swing as high as I dared, intoxicated by the wonders of my magic kingdom.

Several years after grandpa died, we sold the house to a young, just-married couple, probably in much the same way that grandpa and his wife Martha bought it decades earlier. When I drive by now, the garage and

Little House are gone, as are the willows, pond and barn. And the parcel on which it all sat seems soooo very small ... because it is, and always had been.

We chart the "growing up" process by visible signs that mark the transformation of boys and girls into men and women ... first step, first word, first day of school, first puppy love, etc.

Only with hindsight can we recognize the metamorphosis that takes place out of everyone's view as we trade the cocoon of fantasy for the wings of reality.

While we're busy inhabiting the fantasy world of our youth, we can't wait to "grow up." And when we finally do, we often find ourselves longing to return to that simpler time, to the "good old days." I've taken a lot of those trips.

It's almost that time of year again.

Late July and August herald the approach of my favorite season, autumn.

The days are already growing shorter, the sky is taking on an increasingly pale luster and fog is becoming a regular nighttime visitor. Early morning traffic will soon be interrupted by the flashing red lights of school buses. High school bands will fill the afternoon air with symphonies from their practice while football teams gird for Friday night battles under the lights.

A couple of weeks ago, it was a slow afternoon in the office and I had a piece of leftover business in Brookville I'd been saving for such a day.

Satisfied that the trip was warranted, I drove, not west on Interstate 80 but along the Airport Road west of Falls Creek. I turned off Route 830 along the ridge top then went through Allens Mills and Hazen into Brookville.

The "business" took about 30 minutes to conduct. The trip back to DuBois took years to complete.

As I made my way back through Hazen on Route 28,

trying to obey the 35 mph speed limit, I turned left before I got to Nosker Lumber and took the long back way to Brockway through Richardsville and Munderf, over the Game School Road and into Brockway on the Clay Plant Road.

Twenty-some years ago, I was a frequent traveler over these roads. Many times, as afternoon gave way to dusk, my great-grandfather (Bubba), great-grandmother and I would finish supper and sit back and relax.

After a few minutes in his favorite rocker, Bubba would often use his cane to rap on the top drawer in the bureau in the dining room. In that drawer, in a metal box, was a collection of change - nickels, dimes and quarters - that paid for a passport to some of the most wonderful days of my boyhood.

Following orders, I would get a dollar or so in change from that box and Bubba and I would make our way to the garage, he limping from years of grueling work at the Clay Co., me skipping along carefree. The wooden doors of the garage were propped open and the old, red four-door Ford was extracted, ready for takeoff on another adventure.

The roads haven't changed much, if at all, in all these years. Clay Plant is still straight, narrow and bumpy but a nice, comfortable kind of bumpy. The Game School Road still winds past the late Tom Marshall's farm, where hundreds of deer used to roam, then makes its way through a canopy of trees, past the road to the old Game School, which the state closed for a still inexplicable reason some years ago, past the Munderf church and the graveyard behind it, where smooth, polished black tombstones dating to the 1800s still stand.

Then, our destination: Allshouse's Store where, as Bubba was fond of saying, you could find anything from "soup to nuts." What we found usually amounted to an ice cream

Nick Hoffman

sandwich for Bubba and a Fudgsicle for me. *Grandma often settled for a bite of either.*

Those were the days. The fields, the pale late summer and early autumn sky, the shadows. The drive back from Brookville jogged all those little-boy senses to life again. The quarter century or so that's passed melted away and the past and present merged for a few brief, invigorating moments.

Years later, when I got my driver's license, I returned the favor. Bubba was my passenger as we traversed the back roads between Brockway and Brookville. We stopped at Temple Cemetery to let Grandma know we remembered.

Bubba's last ride came in November 1980 and I was there for that one, too, as a mourner. Now, he lies beside Grandma, not far from that faraway land they unlocked for a little boy who still hasn't grown up and who, hopefully, never will.

Rebel With A Cause

When I was in 5th grade, Mrs. Dorothy Moore, my homeroom teacher, polled the class and asked us what we wanted to be when we grew up. I said, without hesitation, "President of the United States." Believe it or not, I was the only one with that career goal.

"Come down to earth, boy," she said in her Scottish brogue.

I relented. A little. "OK. I want to be a U.S. Senator!"

From that day until the Class of 1979 graduated, I was known as "Senator Hoffman."

There must have been a lot going on in my mind in 5th grade. That's also when I decided it was time to educate my classmates on the "facts of life."

I don't recall where the notion was born, but I knew that in order to deliver the goods, I had to find a book about it.

In Brockway, Mengle Memorial Library was the repository of all knowledge. It was named after Glenn Mengle, who was president of Brockway Glass in its heyday in the 1950s and '60s when it became the second largest glass container manufacturer in the world.

I routinely ensconced myself in the reading section, where I voraciously read every newspaper and periodical I could get my hands on.

Nick Hoffman

What I needed to know about the birds and the bees wasn't going to come from a periodical, though. That information was found in reference books, and those were kept behind the front desk. The head librarian said I was too young for that information and wouldn't let me borrow the book.

So I borrowed one from Mr. Reckner, an elementary teacher whose room was next to Mrs. Moore's. Despite a less than thorough understanding of the subject, I managed to produce a credible report, complete with appropriate illustrations on the blackboard.

I was growing up faster than I realized, immersed in the Wonder Years, which I would recall many times over the years. I was also nurturing something of an "anti-establishment" attitude. Not long after the "Senator Hoffman" and "birds and bees" episodes, I found myself challenging authority in a nearby county seat.

• • •

I learned only last week of the Oct. 7 death of retired Elk County Judge Paul B. Greiner.

The obituary didn't run in our newspaper and my occasional checks of neighboring publications didn't catch it.

Judge Greiner became a senior judge when he retired from the Court of Common Pleas, which saw him doing double duty since Elk and Cameron counties are a combined judicial district.

The last time I saw Judge Greiner, probably seven or eight years ago, he said he was busier as a retired senior judge than he'd ever been on the "regular" bench.

State law requires judges to retire at age 70 and I still don't understand why. Former Clarion County Judge Charles

Alexander is a senior judge, as is former Jefferson County Judge Edwin L. Snyder. If they're still good enough to sit on the bench as "retired" judges, they're still good enough for me any day of the week.

My first meeting with Judge Greiner was the most memorable and coincided with one of my early coups against bureaucrats.

One summer day in 1973 or '74, I accompanied my grandmother to the late Dr. James Minteer's office in Ridgway. While she was otherwise occupied, I skipped down to the courthouse, a block or two away, to look at some criminal records in the Prothonotary's Office.

No particular records, just something to do with crime. I was enamored of the law then and wanted to be a lawyer when I grew up.

I walked into the office and requested the records, nothing in particular, thank you.

The clerk, a middle-age woman, was the stuff of which stereotypes are made.

I was too young, she said, to see any of the records I'd asked for.

I have a right to see them, I countered.

Not while I'm here, she said as she handed me some naturalization records instead.

Knowing I was right, I went upstairs to the judge's office. It happened to be lunchtime and his secretary was gone just then.

I knocked on the door to his chambers and walked in. He was seated at a large table with a number of important looking men.

Somewhat annoyed but nonetheless polite, he asked how he could help me.

I told him how I'd been denied access to records I believed (knew) I had every right to see.

Nick Hoffman

He agreed, interrupted whatever he was doing, picked up the phone, called the Prothonotary's Office and left no doubt that I was to be given access to whatever records I was asking for.

When I returned to the office, the woman glared at me and said, "You went to the top echelon. That takes a lot of nerve."

I nodded, trying not to gloat.

And then she handed me the records.

Ironically, the records were of criminal cases but they were juvenile records from the 1940s and juvenile records, no matter how old, are supposed to be sealed forever.

The records paled in comparison to "winning" that battle against the "tyranny and oppression of grownups and the secrecy of government." Remember, Watergate was in full bloom at that time.

Actually, Judge Greiner gave life to an important concept that day: The law applies to everyone equally, the law said those were public records and I was part of the public. That day, even though I probably didn't know it, I trusted grownups and government a little bit more.

All because Judge Greiner took time to listen.

Dear Nicky, ...
I Love You Very Much

Even as I approach 60, nothing has happened to change my conviction that the toughest years are the adolescent ones.

"The Wonder Years" was an ABC Television show about the coming of age of Kevin Arnold (Fred Savage) in suburban America from 1968-73. The title could mean several things:

- The world is full of wonders (it is).
- Teenagers spend a lot of time "wondering" what it's all about (we did).
- We wondered while we wandered (or vice versa), dazed and confused.

Like most kids in the '70s, I easily identified with Kevin Arnold's world ... the names were changed to protect the innocent. ☺

Dad got settled in Colorado and remarried in 1973. His wife Patti had three children by her first marriage: Todd, Brett and Audra. Dad and Patti welcomed a daughter, Jenni Jo, to the tribe in 1974.

Mom remarried in 1973, too. Jim was 12 years younger

than she. In hindsight, their relationship was doomed from the start. Even though they both worked - she as a secretary at Brockway Glass and he at an auto parts dealer - they struggled, living paycheck to paycheck. Mom was a spender of money – whether she had it or not.

That influenced my approach to finances. I got a $2 allowance each week - if they had the money to pay it. I worked to save 50 cents a week - along with birthday money - so I could buy a couple shares of Brockway Glass stock. I bought my first two shares in April 1975 for around $15 each through Parker Hunter in Pittsburgh, arranged by Jean Rittenhouse at Brockway Citizens Bank. I was very proud of those purchases, and the management it took to make them.

We moved from a trailer on Evergreen Avenue to a house on Pershing Avenue in 1974-75. Dad stayed in touch with me, my brother and sister and did everything he could to be a Dad from a distance. He and I worked hard and kept our relationship intact through the years, sharing laughter as well as tears.

Despite the distances that have separated us, Dad exerted the main parental influence in my life. And still does.

About 10 years ago, while I was visiting him in Omaha, we and several of our golfing buddies took a trip to play some courses around Manhattan, Kan., "K State" country.

The crown jewel of our excursion would be the Colbert Hills course at Kansas State,

It was a beautiful morning for golf. For me, it was a beautiful day to commit hara kiri, and I would have if I hadn't dulled the blades on my irons with so many ineffectual swings. THIS was what I rode 3 hours and 166 miles for?! I was having a terrible day. I either needed to hit the reset button on the day, or buy a bushel of mulligans to finish my round while I still had some balls in my bag. Instead, I got an attitude adjustment.

The 9th hole is a "modest" 361-yard par 4. Doglegging left, it is bordered by water and marshy darkness on the left and a grassy mound the entire length of the right side. I chopped my tee shot onto that mound. I had to swing my golf club like a baseball bat to hit the ball, which was about shoulder high. As expected, I whiff-shanked it farther right, so far right that it was closer to the parking lot than the green.

Dad caught up to me in our cart and asked where my ball was. I waved my hand and arm to the right, signaling that it was "outta here!"

"Did you hit another one?" he asked.

"No," I said, plopping my butt down on the seat. "Gimme a 6 (Equitable Stroke Control). That's enough."

I was acting like a petulant child throwing a tantrum and I didn't particularly care who saw it.

But Dad did.

As we finished the front 9, he told me I had 5 minutes to make up my mind to either continue playing and act like a grownup or go back to the hotel while he finished the round. He wasn't going to let me ruin the day for everyone.

We ended up playing 36 holes that day and had a blast. Later, I marveled at how my father, in his early 70s at the time, was unwilling to allow his 40-something son to act like that unchallenged. Before I went to bed, I apologized and thanked him for challenging me. Golf is only a game, after all. Life is the bigger prize.

Dan Fogelberg's music has always resonated with me. When I hear "Leader of the Band," I think of my Dad, especially these lines:

Nick Hoffman

From top left to bottom right: Dad, Nick & Papa

He earned his love through discipline,
a thundering velvet hand
His gentle means of sculpting souls
took me years to understand

I thank you for the kindness and the
times when you got tough
And papa, I don't think I said I love you near enough

The leader of the band is tired and
his eyes are growing old
But his blood runs through my instrument
and his song is in my soul

My life has been a poor attempt to imitate the man
I'm just a living legacy to the leader of the band

That's just the kind of man my Dad is, and always has been.

When he got settled in Denver, Dad wrote me a letter and told me in so many words that I had to be "the man of the house" now. It was dated Saturday, Sept. 9, 1972.

Hello, Nicky,

How are you? How's the weather back there? How are things going in school? I suppose you are getting settled down into the routine by now and getting involved with your new subjects.

Nicky, you are getting old enough now – just think, you'll be 11 years old before long - that you must learn to practice a lot of self-discipline. By that I mean that the older a person gets the more details of life you get exposed to and have to make decisions about. And this is where it is important to be your own man and don't let others influence you.

There are a lot of kids your age who don't take anything

Nick Hoffman

seriously because they have never been taught respect. I know you know what is right but sometimes everyone has weak moments when they don't use their good judgment. You are going to be faced with situations in school when your good judgment will be tested.

Other kids will be doing something that is wrong and they will want you to join them. And even though you know it is wrong you will be tempted to go along with them so they won't call you a chicken or a sissy.

I'm going to tell you a good way to overcome the temptation to join them. I think you've probably seen that commercial on TV that has a "phantom" police car that drivers are supposed to imagine nearby when they are tempted to break a traffic law. Well, when you are on the bus, or at school, or really just anywhere and are tempted to do something you know is wrong just to go along with the gang, you look over your shoulder and pretend that your mother and I and Nan and Poppa are standing there with you. And if it is something that you know we wouldn't like, something that you would be ashamed of or sorry for if you knew we were there – then think twice and don't do it.

Remember son, you never have to be ashamed of doing the RIGHT thing. You can be proud and hold your head high – no matter what the rest of the kids say. Feel sorry for them that they don't know enough to be good like you.

And Nicky, if your imagination isn't good sometimes and you can't see Mom and I and Nan and Poppa there – you KNOW that GOD is always there – and you don't want to disappoint Him either, do you?

I'm telling you this now son because, as I said, the older you get the more tests and trials you will have to face and if you get in the habit of doing the right thing now it will be easier in the future.

I'm sorry I can't be with you. I miss you very much.

But the distance between us does not lessen my love and concern for you. God has blessed you with a good mind. Show Him your appreciation for it by using it the way He and all those on earth who love you would want you to.

I am very proud of you and I want you to get the best grades you are capable of in school and to build a good reputation for behavior. You will find that it will make your later life a lot brighter and more successful.

Also, Nicky, be a good boy for your Mother for she has a big job what with working every day and having to do everything for you and Penny and Kevin. Help her as much as you can and one of the best ways to help her is to always listen and do what she tells you.

*You also should set a good example for your sister and brother because you are older and they will look up to you and do as you do. It's a big job but I know you can handle it son. All of my love to you and remember you are always in my thoughts. Until I see you again, remember - always live for God and your family and you will never fail." **Dad***

Forgive And Forget?

What mom wanted was support money, which Dad didn't have very often. He had his hands full in Denver with a wife and four children. But that didn't stop mom from having the three of us call Dad on weekends, say hello and then ask when he was going to send some money.

To make matters worse, mom concocted a narrative that Dad "deserted" us. I knew better – I was in the kitchen when he said good-bye, remember - and was old enough to realize that mom had a way of creating her own truth to suit situations and could be an accomplished liar when she had to be.

I tried to love my mother, but it wasn't easy because I didn't always like her. I especially dreaded her birthday and Christmas. Finding suitable cards was never easy. I could not bring myself to sign my name to a card that gushed, "Mom, you've always been there for me and I love you so much," or "Thanks, Mom, for all the joy of Christmas when I was growing up." I don't remember love and joy being part of it.

I unloaded the guilt over feeling like that a long time ago. Love and respect are reciprocal. You have to give one to get the other. She made her choices, and lived with the consequences.

In fairness, I eventually realized that some of the trouble I had saying "I love you" came from using my relationship with Dad as a measuring stick. That doesn't work. Each relationship is unique and has to succeed or fail on its own merits and the willingness of the participants to make it work.

Even so, my overriding feeling is one of pity at how shallow and superficial mom could be, of how much she could have contributed to others and how little she actually did. I tried to give her the benefit of the doubt; she wanted to do the right thing, but too often couldn't or wouldn't. The right thing is rarely the easy thing to do.

There's a lesson there for me. I have to remind myself to be on guard in case that recessive gene is part of my DNA, too.

When mom died suddenly at the age of 71 in 2011, I tried to organize those conflicted thoughts in the eulogy I delivered at her funeral, which occurred on the day before Easter.

I don't know how often, or even if Mom, in her private moments and thoughts, reflected on her life. Do any of us?

Maybe that's because when we look in the rear view mirror at our lives, our attention is drawn to the negatives.

What did I do that I shouldn't have done? What should I have done that I didn't?

If we allow ourselves to sink into a well of despair, life is content to let us wallow there.

Let's look at life in baseball terms. That's fitting because Mom was a scorekeeper for the Rovers at Brockway High School for Coach Harry Pinge.

Life tossed its share of nasty curve balls at Mom. And she swung at some bad pitches. She's not alone on either score, even though I think she was sometimes convinced that she was. She booted a couple balls. Tripped a few

Nick Hoffman

times rounding the bases. Haven't each of us? Our faults and frailties are part of what makes us human.

Near the end of the 71st inning, she made it home Wednesday. I believe the Umpire called her "Safe!" And His calls are the ones that count.

We tend to judge ourselves harshly, either by over-emphasizing our failings or underestimating our worth.

God's willingness to look beyond our humanness is what makes Him God.

Many years ago, a group of people mourned the death of their son, brother and friend.

Like us, they felt loss and despair and were griefstricken at the finality of death.

They did not know that the sorrow of that evening would be wiped away the next morning; that death's sting would be forever muted.

I do not believe it is an accident that we say our final goodbyes to Mom today. In God's perfect timing, there are no accidents or coincidences.

We know that the son, brother and friend whom they mourned those many years ago was Jesus Christ. They could not have any inkling that He would be raised and, with His resurrection, all of mankind – and yes, that includes each of us – has had hope of eternal life.

Today, on the eve of Easter, we share that hope, embrace it and are comforted by it.

The weight of life without hope was lifted. Death was revealed for what the psalmist called it centuries before ... the shadow of death.

Surely, on that day between Good Friday and Easter Sunday, which happens to be today, it must have seemed as if the ball game was over.

We know better.

Each of us, no matter what it looks like in the rear view

mirrors of our lives, has worth. We need look no further than that lonely cross and that empty tomb for proof.

For God so loved the world ... for God so loved each and every one of us.

A perfect game is a rare but doable feat in baseball. Not so in life.

But there is good news ... we don't have to be perfect.

What we have to be is willing ... willing to admit our shortcomings, willing to acknowledge the unearned favor of a loving God, willing to accept the salvation of a risen Savior.

The pain of this moment will pass. The game will go on until, one by one, each of us rounds third base and heads for home.

I pray that each of us will make that final turn with God standing in the coach's box, urging us on.

The Apostle Paul - surely as flawed and seemingly unfit for service to God as one could imagine but who ended up writing a good bit of the New Testament - talked about running the race - about rounding those bases - in Philippians 3:13-14.

I pray that we can find comfort - and hope - in his words as we go from here.

"... but one thing I do, forgetting those things that are behind and reaching forward to those things that are ahead, I press toward the goal for the prize of the upward call of God in Christ Jesus."

I Never Had Any Friends Later On ...

I was making friends and starting to "fit in" by the time I reached junior high. Many of those friendships lasted beyond high school, and one in particular was very special then and has remained so ever since.

"I never had any friends later on like the ones I had when I was twelve. .... does anyone?"

That's the last "line," typed onto a computer screen in the 1986 movie "Stand by Me." It's the story of four boys who venture into the Oregon wilderness on Labor Day weekend in search of Ray Brower, a missing boy. They eventually find him dead along the railroad tracks, having been hit by a train.

I thought about those words and that movie as I sat in St. Tobias Church in Brockway at the funeral Mass for Nancy Olivio. Her oldest son, Jim, co-starred with me in our very own production of "Stand by Me" in the mid-1970s at Brockway Area High School.

Jim's father, Richard, died in 1973, when Jim was 12 or 13. A year earlier, my parents divorced and Dad moved to Denver.

Jim and I met in 1974. He was playing junior high basketball for Perk Binney. I was the team's manager.

We quickly became friends and I met the rest of his family, including Nancy. I wasn't introduced to the family as much as I was absorbed into it. Jim's grandparents – his father's parents - lived next door and operated a greenhouse. Across the parking lot was Genevro's Inn, which led to my absorption into that family, since one of Fino's and Flora's sons, Dave, was one of Jim's best friends … and mine, too.

We never made a wilderness pilgrimage looking for missing persons, but we sure did share some times. Looking back through the mists of 40 years ago, we didn't spend much if any time talking about what we didn't have or what we'd been through. Some of our innocence might have been rubbed away but our resilience was intact.

Jim endured. We endured. That's the way it was. Cars, like his burgundy Monte Carlo or Dave's green Cutlass or my blue Grenada, had rear view mirrors. We were too busy looking forward to look back. Life was still largely carefree and in front of us. We took advantage of that grace.

Ultimately, our paths diverged; Jim worked as a mouldmaker for 30 years and, after that, an electrician. He and his wife Connie raised two fine sons, Kyle and Jordan.

I married a newspaper and nurtured that relationship for 30 years before I moved on. We saw less of each other, but that didn't dull our relationship. We are still best friends. When we did touch base, outside of birthday and Christmas cards, we marveled at how little we saw of each other but how close we remained.

I was at the funeral Masses for his grandparents, too, and for his younger brother Danny, who died in 2005. He was there for me when my grandparents and my Mom died. He held me in his arms as I cried like a baby after my Grandpa died.

The songs at Friday's Mass – "Amazing Grace," "The Prayer of St. Francis" and "How Great Thou Art" – are

Nick Hoffman

guaranteed to pry me open like a can of tuna fish. As I
alternately sang and wept, I looked at Jim, shoulders back,
carrying the mantel of eldest son. I looked through the mist
and saw the curly haired boy who became my best friend.
And I was proud of him.

Msgr. Charles Kaza paid tribute to the faith and
endurance that Nancy had in raising four children after
her husband's death, working full-time, enduring Danny's
death and always giving, doing, serving.

Our culture is increasingly obsessed with measuring
the success of someone's life. For me, the question should
be how meaningful our lives are, how much of a difference
they make in someone else's life.

I remembered Nancy. I looked at Jim. I didn't have to
look any further for the answer.

"I never had any friends later on like the ones I had when
I was twelve."

On the home front, the reality sank in that I wasn't the
man of the house. Jim and mom fell in love with racing, and
that meant, like it or not, I spent most Saturday evenings
in the summer at the Clearfield Speedway and most
Sunday afternoons at the drag strip in New Bethlehem.
I hated every minute of it; a seething hate that is rarely
forgiven and never forgotten.

Things got even tougher one afternoon in early 1975.
Jim and I had a huge, nasty blow-up. It was bad. I fled
to the safety of Nan and Papa's house. As things turned
out, it was the pardon that changed everything for a few
years.

When I told mom what happened, it was obvious that
this was a "not enough room for the both of us" situation
and I was the odd man out. It was equally obvious that her

needs were going to come first. Mom was always whining about "getting the dirty end of the stick."

So, despite me being her son, Jim stayed and I moved in with Nan and Papa.

I realized years later that something that could have damaged me permanently ended up being a blessing in disguise. There's a verse, Genesis 50:20 that says, in part, "You meant evil against me, but God meant it for good, in order to bring it about as it is this day." That was the first, but not the last, time that happened.

Mom and Jim suffered through a rocky relationship and finally separated in November 1977. I happened to be at the house the night he packed his things and left. Despite what had happened between us, I couldn't hate him, either. The last thing I said to him was, "I love you."

Less than a month later, on Sunday evening, Dec. 4, 1977, Papa and I were watching an NFL football game on TV. The phone rang. It was Mom. Jim's parents had returned home from a weekend getaway. They found Jim dead at their home. He was 26.

Nick Hoffman

Play It Again, Papa

Nan was the only daughter and one of three children (sons Sam and William "Wee Wee") of Jack and Martha Repiscak.

Papa was one of five boys and six children of William and Katherine Hoffman. His father was a railroad man, based in Corry, not far from Erie.

But Papa grew up in Brockway and not until more than 10 years after his death did Nan and I learn "the rest of the story."

Our family home was built by Redford "Pa" Segers, a sawyer from Maine who was drawn to Brockway by the allure of the timber industry in our part of Pennsylvania in the years immediately following the Civil War.

He bought a 70-acre tract along what is now U.S. Route 219 east of Brockway and built a 14-room, three-story Victorian mansion.

Pa Segers was married twice. Frone and Mabel were daughters from his second marriage. A daughter from his first marriage married into the Rhed family. Her daughter Katherine married William Hoffman. So rather than "being given away," Papa – the great-grandson of Pa Segers - was entrusted to his mother's aunts. Mabel died in 1938. When Frone died in 1945, Nan and Papa and their 7-year-old son – my Dad - moved into the house on

Aug. 14, V-J Day, the day the Japanese surrendered and World War II finally came to an end.

Periodically, there is a confluence of meaningful dates in my life, and 2010 happens to be one of those years.

This week is Holy Week, the holiest of weeks for Christians, the one that seized victory from the grave and took away death's sting in one stunning instant on the first Easter.

This week also marks the 29th anniversary of my grandfather's death. Coincidentally or not, that date and Good Friday fall on April 2 this year.

Papa was only 63 when the combination of two heart attacks, the effects of a four-pack-a-day cigarette habit and pneumonia overcame him.

One of six children, born in 1917 along with a twin brother, he was too sickly to return with his parents and family to Waterford, where his father worked as a railroad engineer, and was raised by two aunts, both single school teachers, Frone and Mabel Segers, in the family home north of Brockway.

Growing up apart from his parents couldn't have been easy, but any pain he felt was wallpapered over with the "little" things in life ... mowing grass, painting, bowling, commiserating (one of his favorite words, and pastimes) over a cup of coffee, golfing or sitting beside a fire in the back yard under a black walnut tree and listening to Pittsburgh Pirates games.

Our basement was his laboratory, from whence came, among other things, the gaudy orange front door that made my Grandmother's blood pressure spike, and the snow shovel he cobbled together from an old coal stove shovel and a too-thick, 6-foot tall pole that made his brother-in-law's and sister-in-law's jaws drop when he emerged from the catacombs and unveiled it.

After any or all of those endeavors were over, he'd sit up late ("early to bed" was NOT in his repertoire) until programming ended and the test patterns took over, rising occasionally for a cup of coffee or a bowl of ice cream, and whacking the television set on his way past to stop the picture from rolling.

He was also a piano player, and I remember him seated at the piano in the hallway belting out any number of tunes.

Piano playing is not genetic. I can't play a note, although I learned to stroke a computer keyboard as well as he knew how to play the keys on that piano.

His presence and counsel filled the holes in my teenage years with substance and direction, even if I did stray from time to time.

I stood at the foot of his hospital bed in Ridgway on the morning of April 2, 1981. I was 19 ... and I knew that this was good-bye. I needed him then. I need him today. I'll always need him. And because of who he was and what he left behind – the love and lessons – I'll always have him.

I'll mark this Friday – Good Friday – as the day two of the most influential and important people in my life died.

Then, Sunday, I'll celebrate the resurrection of the One that gave the other – and all of us – eternal hope.

Papa's favorite tune on the piano was "Ah! Sweet Mystery of Life."

I can still hear the notes – he didn't sing the words – DA da dadada dad a dad a da DA DA!

Through the miracle of Google, I found the lyrics and understood why it was his favorite.

> Ah! Sweet mystery of life
> At last I've found thee
> Ah! I know at last the
> secret of it all;

*All the longing, seeking,
striving, waiting, yearning
The burning hopes, the
joy and idle tears that fall!*

*For 'tis love, and love
alone, that can repay!
'Tis the answer, 'tis the
end and all of living
For it is love alone that
rules for aye!*

*Love, and love alone, the
world is seeking,
For 'tis love, and love
alone, that can repay!*

*'Tis the answer, 'tis the
end and all of living
For it is love alone that rules for aye!*

Play it again, Papa.

Walburn Runs Through It

O ur mailing address used to be RD3, Box-something-or-other. Then 911 addressing came along and it was something-something Route 219. Google Maps will provide the exact coordinates.

But if you listen closely, you can "hear" where home is.

"Eventually, all things merge into one, and a river runs through it."

So wrote Norman Maclean in the novel and, later, movie by the same name, "A River Runs Through It." It is about his youth in Montana. The Big Blackfoot River was the object of Maclean's affection, the eternal constant in the changing times of World War I, Prohibition and the Great Depression during which he grew to manhood.

I think about Maclean and the Big Blackfoot once in a while during what have become frequent walks along a run, Walburn by name, to whose banks I am drawn. Walburn Run has its origins, according to local lore and Google maps, in two like-named tributaries that emanate in the wilderness between Brockway and the gamelands of southern Elk County.

They do not yield to lines etched on man's maps nor have they heeded his commands. The branches merge into a singular Walburn Run and, not unlike the begets and begats of the Old Testament, its waters flow into Toby Creek and Toby feeds the Clarion River and the Clarion begets or is begotten of the Allegheny River until it intersects with the Monongahela to form the Ohio which feeds the Mighty Mississippi and, ultimately, the Gulf.

Walburn Run is officially birthed near where I turn around on my now 2.8-mile sojourn and head for home. Except I don't "live" there anymore, in the 14-room home my great-great-great-grandfather Redford "Pa" Segers, a lumberman and shipbuilder from Maine, built when he helped pioneer this valley in the latter half of the 19th century.

But Walburn Run will always be "home" and even though my head has hit the pillow in DuBois these last six years, it is along Walburn, on the best of days and the worst and all those between, that I am most alive. The waters of Walburn Run formed the eastern boundary of our property, but we spoke of it as "the creek," pronounced "crick," just like the occasional pain in the neck, in a dialect unique to Western Pennsylvania.

Walburn Run is also what we called the road that runs alongside the wet Walburn Run once we crossed Route 219 north of Brockway. But our Walburn Run Road was an unnamed township thoroughfare until the advent of 911 addressing dubbed it McCain Street, even though, as any local will tell you, McCain runs off Main Street at the corner by Aunt Helen's old house, then up Cemetery Hill to St. Tobias Cemetery, where we laid her to rest at the age of 95.

In point of fact, the real Walburn Run Road begins at young Ralph Reed's house and meanders back to Charnisky Drive near the Rev. Dave Nagele's church, back where Walburn Run - the wet - begins. Nomenclature aside, there are photos of my Dad and Mom taking me for walks along Walburn Run by day, before they tightened the braces into place on my legs by night to try, unsuccessfully, to remedy the bowleggedness that nature endowed me with.

Grandma and I took this walk many times, sharing old memories while making new ones. One day, she tripped and fell on some anti-skid and twisted her wrist. "It's broken," I said. "It is not," she protested. "It is," the doctor said.

There are spots along my walk where the waters of Walburn are not visible, engulfed by the wetlands she nourishes on her way south. Then, not far from a giant gnarled oak that stands sentinel along the road, she breaks into view. And before I see her, I hear her water gurgling as it, as Maclean described, "runs over rocks from the basement of time."

It is a walk for all seasons. My favorite is autumn, sunlight glistening on and through the palette of yellow and red and orange that adorns the trees on the hillsides that embrace this placid valley in a timeless hug. The same sunlight that sparkled like diamonds one frosty morn not long ago when the temperature hovered in the teens.

I do not have to see Walburn Run. I hear birds chirping and the soft echo of leaves falling to earth and the rustling of squirrels as they prance on the hemlocks or dance on the forest floor. And if I could neither see nor hear it, I can smell it; apples on the trees and apples that have fallen from them - not many this year - or coal burning in furnaces, given away by wisps of smoke rising skyward on fair days or rising then flattening as harbingers of an approaching storm.

It is a walk of solitude rather than a solitary walk; a parade that reaches back to the past and meets the present as the future looms just ahead, a continuum of time interrupted - but never broken - by external events. All that matters to me is here, within reach however briefly. And it always has been, just like the waters of Walburn Run that have flowed, are flowing, are destined to flow for time immemorial. And, to borrow a phrase, a river runs through it.

Coffee And A Movie
With Papa

The house that Pa Segers built is where we lived from the time I was born until Dad and Mom divorced in 1972. I moved back there in 1975 and remained until I went to college at Penn State's main campus in University Park in 1981.

Nan lived there alone after Papa died in 1981. I returned in 1992, seeking a respite from the mess I was making of my life. It was more house than she needed. The upper two floors were shut off and slowly decaying. The front porch had rotted. The roof was leaking. She was ready to sell it when I intervened and invested the money to restore it.

We commissioned David Taylor of Brookville to research the history of the house and were successful in having it placed on the National Register of Historic Places.

It was only then that we found out the rest of the story with respect to how and by whom Papa had been raised. If he knew, he never told a soul, even Nan.

He and Nan eloped to New York State with the help of his uncle, Elton Rhed, in 1937. Papa was 20; Nan was 18. My Dad was born on Jan. 16, 1938.

He and Nan and Dad created a 9-hole par 3 golf course – Tiny Tee - on 9 acres behind the house in the 1960s. It was lighted and became a popular local attraction. It closed in 1971 as other obligations - Dad's bowling alley, Timber Lanes, in Brockway, Nan's mother's declining health and Papa's "day job" in the mould repair shop - left too few people and too little time to stay caught up.

My bedroom was on the second floor. Papa knew my favorite color was blue and he created the Blue Room just for me. He installed a blue carpet, painted the walls and ceiling - and woodwork and desk - blue. We didn't heat the upstairs, which meant I could burrow under a comforter or quilt and enjoy their warm embrace on the coldest night.

There were three windows in the Blue Room. The north-facing one looked out over the front yard, where a gnarled apple tree stood in a corner. I lay in bed on many a moonlit winter night, listening to CBS Radio Mystery Theater with E.G. Marshall on the radio to the moans of the boughs of that tree as they were caressed by a dry, cold north wind.

It sure beat what I'd been delivered from; lying awake listening to beer bottles bounce off the walls while expletives flew.

It's funny how certain things - a song, a sound, a movie - catapult us back into long-ago and faraway moments of our lives, usually when we least expect it.

When I was growing up, I spent a lot of time with my Dad's parents, Ken and Jo Hoffman.

"Papa" worked for 41 years at Brockway Glass. He was Depression-hardened and, along with Grandma, had learned to appreciate what they had, which wasn't always much, rather than moan about what they didn't have.

It's a trait they passed on to me, one I'm grateful for.

Over years of weaning at the kitchen table, where Papa reigned in all of his often shirtless splendor, I learned to appreciate a cup of coffee, muddied with Carnation instant milk and sweetened with two sugars, and a hand of cards.

In the living room, on the black-and white set that Papa often had to rap to keep the picture from rolling, I also learned to enjoy Westerns. TV wasn't an all-night proposition back then. Cable wasn't universally available, either. Whatever late night viewing we did was usually on Channel 6 "Serving millions from atop the Alleghenies." Even on weekends, late night movies only lasted until 2 or 3 a.m., followed by the test pattern.

That was still longer than I usually lasted. Propped up on a couch, my eyelids drooped, then invariably closed before the closing credits rolled across that rolling screen and I'd wake up, get up and trudge off to bed.

"How can you leave in the middle of this good Western?" he'd chide me, smiling.

I'm convinced Papa was part owl, and he would revel in today's 24/7 cable fare. And remote control.

Those days, in many ways the best I've ever known, were cut short when Papa died at age 63 in 1981.

There are two moments I particularly look forward to each week; getting home after work on Friday nights with the weekend in front of me and returning home from church on Sundays, especially during NFL season.

A few weeks ago on a Friday evening, I got home, ate supper, did some paperwork and housework, then made a pot of coffee and prepared to sit down in my recliner and relax.

For no particular reason, I thought how nice it would be to watch "Winchester '73," a watershed blockbuster Western from 1950 starring James Stewart. It is the movie credited with re-popularizing Westerns in the post-World

Nick Hoffman

War II era, and a lot of very fine Westerns were made over the next quarter century - "The Horse Soldiers," "Rio Lobo" and "Shenandoah" among my favorites.

Lo and behold, as I turned to Channel 252 on the Comcast cable that serves DuBois, there it was ... "Winchester '73." Commercial-Free, it runs for an hour and 35 minutes. There's a lot of action packed into those 95 minutes, including a Dodge City rifle shoot, sibling rivalry, outlaws, cavalry, Indians, love, death and frontier justice.

A lot has happened since April 2, 1981, when Papa died in Kittanning, en route to a Pittsburgh hospital. I wish he'd been here for some of it; I'm glad he wasn't for other stuff.

On that Friday night last month, with coffee in hand - cream and sugar of course - we shared "Winchester '73" one more time.

We?

That's right.

I stayed awake and was reminded that even after 27 years, he never left. As long as there's coffee in the pot and a Western on TV, I doubt he ever will.

Nan & Papa and Walburn Run Road

Nick Hoffman

Beautiful Days In The Neighborhood

One casualty of technology and social media has been the presence in our lives of neighbors. Life seemed slow compared to today's pace, and that allowed time to share life with those around us, outside the family.

Such gatherings often took place in the evenings, once supper was finished, when day began fading to dusk but it wasn't quite time to turn in.

Walburn Run and its environs shed a tear Sunday with the news of Irv Keith's passing.

Irv and his wife Janet were fixtures in my lifetime - as well as my Dad's and his parents' - in the house across the street from where I grew up.

Irv will be widely remembered as a businessman, inventor and outdoorsman.

I'll always think of Irv and Janet as neighbors. That's a concept that has become passe in too many places. Not, thankfully, along Walburn Run Road.

Irv and Janet's place is guarded by a phalanx of stately trees in front, including an apple tree on the corner, the boughs casting an umbrella of shade on the front porch.

A sprawling, manicured lawn encircles the house down

to the creek. In the rear are the back porch - and its swing - and Irv's prize garden.

I never got in and out of there on a late summer evening after a bike ride without taking home some of the bounty of the garden to my Grandma. Beans, zucchini, squash and more.

We spent a few hours on that back porch, too, nibbling on Hershey's Kisses and chatting about the weather (too hot or too dry, the varmints (alternately rabbits, deer or groundhogs) or whatever other topic came up.

Irv loved to tinker. His mind was constantly at work and his body followed, never too far behind.

He was always making things and then fine-tuning them. Projects, like life, both works in progress.

A few years ago, Irv and I spent part of a lazy Saturday afternoon "on the pond" near his son Bud's place south of Brockway. The project at the time was a pontoon rowboat and Irv was bound and determined to make an ultra lightweight model.

My first clear recollection of Irv and Janet came at a more urgent and traumatic time. On Aug. 1, 1969, my brother Kevin was injured in a riding mower accident. He was taken to the hospital and the family followed, except for me and my sister Penny. We went across the street with Irv and Janet, safe and secure and comforted.

Irv was 92 and, in the last year or two, the bittersweet ravages of age began to catch up with him to the point where they slowed him down. That took some doing. He was a tough guy to catch and keep up with.

A couple summers ago, on a hot, stifling August night, a thunderstorm swept through the valley. Grandma and I opened the front door to catch a breath of the cool air that descends in a storm's wake.

There, across the road, was Irv, walking slowly from the

mailbox, each step an obvious struggle, as was the climb up the front porch steps.

Grandma, who'd known Irv longer and is somewhat more familiar with the aches and pains of aging than I (even though she's only 82), sighed sympathetically as she watched our neighbor make his way across the lawn.

"Isn't that too bad?" she asked.

"Yes, it is," I said, acknowledging her point but, at the same time, admiring the grit and determination that refused to let him quit, that enabled him to follow one painful step with another unyielding one.

The back porch swing has an empty spot now. But the crickets are still chirping, the wind is still rustling those leaves and Walburn Run Road continues to be lighted by the glow of Irv and Janet's place.

Thank God for neighbors.

Under The Walnut Tree

I've been drinking coffee with cream and sugar for a long time. I don't remember exactly when I started, other than it was while I was in high school. I do know exactly why I started. Because that's what Papa and Wee Wee drank. I couldn't wait to grow up, and drinking coffee with them made me feel more grown up.

Playing cards with them had the same effect. They were inseparable, even though Wee Wee was a hunter and fisherman, two things Papa wasn't.

Neither of them was materially well off either. Both labored in factories to support their families. They – we – had enough, and I began to understand that "enough" meant less of material things and more of time together with each other.

We spent a lot of time together. There was one place in particular where I felt like the world was at our feet and no one had it better than we did.

I have never since found the peace and contentment I knew then. But even the best of times don't last forever.

Wee Wee died Thursday (Nov. 11, 1993). We knew that it was just a matter of time before his eight-year-long battle with cancer ended. The last few days were particularly cruel but, mercifully, it's over.

Wee Wee (William Repiscak) was my great uncle, literally and figuratively. His nickname was a misnomer because Wee Wee was not a small man. He stood 6-foot-4 with elegant, wavy silver hair. He was an imposing man, despite having only one eye, the other lost in a childhood accident. He was born, lived, worked, raised his family and died in Brockway. With his passing, my little Triumvirate has dwindled to me.

My grandfather, Wee Wee's best friend, died 12 years ago. Now, Wee Wee's gone, too. I did a lot of growing up with Papa and Wee Wee. Their friendship was very close, very special. They were more brothers-in-fact than brothers-in-law. Being admitted to membership in that relationship was akin to having the mantel of manhood bestowed.

Long after Tiny Tee miniature golf course near Brockway closed to the public, Papa and Wee Wee and I took our turns swatting faded, cut and out-of-round golf balls over what was left of a very engaging little layout. Papa had his archaic "jigger," something like a sawed-off 2-iron while Wee Wee took his crooked, hickory-shafted 5-iron to do battle. Even with more modern implements of warfare, I was often no match for them.

We took our little show on the road once or twice to the mountains of Cameron County Country Club near Emporium or to the rustic charm of Elk County Country Club in Ridgway. "What are these guys doing here?" I could imagine club golfers asking as they looked on. But to me, it seemed perfectly natural, two men and a boy having a blast.

Papa and Wee Wee were long-time card combatants. They played for hours upon hours, at the kitchen table and at an eight-sided card table in a metal shed heated by two antique kerosene heaters.

Wee Wee may have been the best cinch player to ever

bid four on a bare deuce. In fact, trailing badly against Papa one time, he cinched on a bare jack, made it, and forced Papa's retirement from the game forever. But they played on — Jacks or better, trips to win; five-card and seven-card stud, baseball and others whose names I can no longer recall. Wee Wee made a habit of thrashing three generations of Hoffmans at cards over 40 or 50 years.

Papa, Wee Wee & Bubba

He Was There All the Time

He made a career out of turning bad hands into good ones, often winners. And he laughed all the while. Wee Wee was always laughing, even when it hurt. And that was often. There's a lesson there.

When we weren't flailing away at a golf ball or whiling away hours playing cards, we'd sit under the black walnut tree in the back yard, build a fire and listen to Pittsburgh Pirates baseball radio broadcasts.

The golf course is overrun with weeds now. The cards lie dormant. The fires have smoldered and died and the radio has fallen silent. Strange how much little things like those matter so much and remain so vividly, indelibly etched in our memories as time marches on. I bet the next time I walk past that walnut tree, I'll hear Bob Prince doing a play-by-play with Nellie King, and I'll smell the burning wood, see the glowing embers and feel the damp chill of a late August night. And I'll thank God that I had Papa and Wee Wee. I hope everybody has someone like that. And I pray that they know how very, very lucky they are if they do.

'I'm Sorry' ... Too Little, Too Late

D espite lots of good advice, many of us learn lessons "the hard way" growing up. I guess those are the ones that "stick." I am no exception, but there is one lesson I wish I could have learned a lot easier.

In the wake of the Columbine (Colo.) high school shooting in April 1999, I wrote a column about the "bullying" that was blamed for Eric Harris' and Dylan Klebold's rampage that killed 13 people and wounded 24. Bullying was mostly unchallenged when I was in school, regarded as a "rite of passage."

"No harm, no foul." Right?

I spent some more time Tuesday night pondering the tragedy and thinking back to my days in high school. "They weren't accepted." "People made fun of them." "They wanted revenge."

I was struck again by something that has bothered me about the high school system. It's an unintended consequence, I suppose, of a system that so readily categorizes students based on their abilities into categories such as "academic" or "general" or "business."

Obviously, educators have to have a selection system for identifying students' strengths and weaknesses and helping them capitalize on the former and overcome the latter. Life's just around the corner once you're in ninth grade.

But the classifications set the stage for conflict when one group believes itself to be superior to another. We had it at Brockway Area High School. Throw in the "jocks" and a few other cliques and it's probably a wonder there wasn't more animosity than there was.

I'm not faulting the educators for the system. I was an academic and that course of study prepared me well for a stint at Penn State. But I never did like or master shop class. And, subconsciously at least, I didn't make time for those who excelled in those areas.

Somewhere along the line, I missed sensitivity class. Somehow, we identified with our differences and ignored the similarities, like being kids in a complex world, growing up too fast with too little to hold on to.

Kids have an extraordinary and boundless capacity for cruelty at times; not every time and not in every circumstance. But it's there, never far from the surface, waiting for sufficient provocation. We were no different.

In eighth grade, Bev and I locked horns throughout the year. We didn't like each other, not even a little bit, for no special reason. We were different people who gravitated to different groups and circulated with different people. And every time the opportunity presented itself, we carved each other up with switchblade-like tongues. And we did so with relish. Kids know where the soft spots are.

In science class or study hall, we beat each other up, trying to inflict as much humiliation and pain as we could.

To this day, I don't know why. I'm not even sure there was a why. Just two ships that passed in the night and paused to fire a few shots across each other's bows.

The school year ended and another carefree summer loomed, to be followed by a carefree fall, etc.

It was carefree for me until Sunday, Aug. 24, 1975.

I turned on the noon news to see what was happening and I learned that Bev had died of injuries she suffered in a mini-bike accident two months earlier.

Dead?

Yep, dead.

She was 14.

I was numbed then like I was earlier this week. "I'll never have a chance to set things right," I said to myself. "I didn't mean any of that stuff I said, even if she did mean what she said to me, which I'm not sure she did."

But it was too late.

Too late then. Too late now.

There are moments in each of our lives when we do a lot of growing up in a very short time.

That day was one of those times, for I realized then the finality of death and the futility of cruelty. And it was too late to do anything about either.

I've said and done a lot of things that have hurt too many people since those long-ago, so-called carefree days. But I've added "I'm sorry" to my vocabulary and it's something I've never since been ashamed to say.

I only wish I would have said it one more time.

In The Huddle: The X's and O's

I realized fairly early that I was possessed of an analytical mind. Knowing the "what" of things came easy except for algebra, which will never make sense.

What challenged me was figuring out "why." Once I knew that, life was reduced to applied logic. Simple enough.

I was perplexed by the messages my hormones were bombarding me with. My body was trying to take me places my brain didn't want to go.

At school, I was s-l-o-w-l-y emerging from my cocoon and had made a few good friends, good enough to be hurt when I saw them tormented by strained relationships with their girlfriends.

"Why," I asked myself, "do I want to hurt like that? Can't they see? Love is an illusion."

Add in the turmoil I'd seen on the home front and that conclusion made absolutely perfect sense to me. I felt like Archimedes when he jumped out of the bath and yelled "Eureka," as he ran naked through the streets of Syracuse after discovering the principle of buoyancy.

One line from Bette Midler's 1979 song "The Rose" said it well: *Some say love, it is a razor, that leaves your soul to bleed."* I disconnected mind and body and decided I wouldn't waste my time chasing love. And I didn't. I realize now that as much sense as that decision made when I made it, I didn't have all the facts or the understanding necessary to make it.

At the same time, I also realized that I had to look out for me. I and I alone held the key to my heart, and **nobody** could intrude unless I let them in. Coming from a broken home and with all that had happened since, I didn't want to hurt anymore. I was still a virgin when I graduated high school, but nobody had broken my heart, and avoiding that was my top priority.

Even so, inside my cocoon, a metamorphosis was taking place. From being perhaps the biggest geek in 7th grade, I started down a winding road over the ensuring six years that included being Junior Class president, No. 1 Varsity golfer my senior year, named "most likely to succeed" by my classmates and the anchor speaker at graduation.

I have practically no athletic ability but that didn't stop me from being a sports fan. The Pittsburgh Steelers were winning Super Bowls then and everybody was a fan. Playing isn't the only way to participate, I soon found out.

Almost without exception coaches in those days were faculty members. Coaches spent more time with many of their players than the kids' parents did. And coaches knew who was having trouble in class ... or fighting with a girlfriend ... or doing things they shouldn't be ... or going through torment at home.

Times change. If it weren't for the number of non-faculty coaches today, a lot of sports programs wouldn't exist. But the stabilizing influence a coach who was also

He Was There All the Time   53

a teacher could and did make a difference in lives ... including mine.

The first coach to take notice of me was Charlie Zoffuto, a business teacher and also the head football coach. He dispatched one of his manager-trainers, my classmate Jeff Pisarcik, to enlist me to the Rovers sideline.

Practice started on the second Monday in August with double-day practices. That was usually the hottest part of summer. I felt like Gunga Din! Doling out water and salt tablets enhanced my popularity, and boosted my confidence.

Our main supplier of athletic supplies was Cramer Sports Medicine - gauze, tape and three shades of analgesic balm with which so much lockerroom mischief was made. Coach Frank Foulkrod urged me to take the Cramer course and become a trainer. Doing so added to my value on the team.

During the same period, the hometown weekly newspaper, the Brockway Record, was looking for a sportswriter. Dad had written for the Record and, later, the Courier-Express. I had a reputation as a good writer and was asked if I'd be interested. Well, yeahhhh, since I had the best seat in the house from which to cover games.

Many high school teams played Saturday afternoon games. We might have two or three night games away from home in a season, and they were "treats," but Saturday afternoons left a lasting impression on me. So did Coach Zoffuto.

It is only fitting that when the time came for Charlie Zoffuto to check in at the great lockerroom in the sky, he did it on the day classes began at his old stomping grounds, Brockway Area High School.

That day came Tuesday when Coach died at age 85.

A business teacher by profession, he was a football and wrestling coach by instinct.

I worked under coach as a manger, trainer and statistician for the Rover football team in the mid- and late 1970s.

At that point in my life, I needed to belong to something. Coach must've sensed that because he recruited and, finally, badgered me into lending a helping hand.

Oh, those glorious days on the sidelines on a sunny Saturday afternoon at Taylor Memorial Field in Brockway, bathed in sunlight filtered through azure skies while the nip of fall chilled the air and the band pounded out "The Horse" as the players pounded on each other.

I can close my eyes even now and taste those delightful days.

My only contact with Coach as a teacher was in typing class in my freshman year. My Mom refused to sign my curriculum sheet unless I took typing. Less than enthusiastic then, I can't imagine life without it now.

Up in the 200 Wing at the high school, Coach stalked the aisles between the desks while his students pounded out "asdf;lkj" on yellow paper on manual typewriters.

As a coach, as much as he would growl on occasion, he asked only of his players to give it all they had. If it wasn't enough to win, it was still good enough for him. Try to get away with less than your best, though, and Coach and you had a problem.

Of course, Coach was the sole arbiter of whether we were giving our best regardless of what we thought.

The wins may not have come as frequently as any of us would have liked, although he guided us to the Little 12 title game in the 1977 season, his last at the helm, against (future NFL Hall of Fame member) Jim Kelly's East Brady Bulldogs, the only team to beat us that year.

Kelly & Co. prevailed, 27-6, but we gave it all we had, even in defeat.

Some of us, the lucky ones, learned as years passed that giving your best applies to a bigger and more substantial playing field than the gridiron.

I remember a Friday afternoon at the field, preparing for Saturday's game with a light workout. Joe Petak was having trouble kicking field goals.

Coach lectured, scolded and instructed Joe on the proper technique, but to no avail.

Finally, at wit's end Coach, a placekicker himself then in his mid-60s, told Joe to step aside. He lined up, called for the snap and "step," "plant," "kick" sent the ball soaring through the uprights.

"Do as I say AND as I do," Coach said, without saying a word.

When Coach left the sidelines for the final time, he turned the reins over to his trusted assistant, Bert Riggle, who guided the Rovers to glory in the same quiet partnership with players that Zoffuto tried to mold.

The last time I saw Coach was at Bert's funeral a couple years ago.

I was sitting in a pew at the Presbyterian Church in Brockway when I felt a hand, or more precisely a paw, on my shoulder.

I turned and saw Coach for the first time in years, since he and his wife Della moved to Indiana (Pa.) to enjoy their retirement.

"Coach," I said, "You look great!"

And he did. Really.

"Sure I do," he shot back with that wry smile and dry, acerbic tone.

That was Coach, right or wrong, direct and to the point. Just like that kick so many years ago.

The title song for the movie by the same name, "The Way We Were," captured the magic of those days in the mid- and late 1970's:

*Memories may be beautiful and yet
What's too painful to remember
We simply choose to forget.
So it's the laughter we will remember
Whenever we remember
The way we were.
The way we were.*

Under His Wings

Coach Zoffuto took care of my autumns. What of winter?

Another classmate, Bobby Schlemmer, asked if I wanted to sign on as a manager for the boys' basketball team and Coach John McNulty. Of course I did.

Until the day he died more than 30 years later, he was "Coach." And a lot more than that.

Born in Philadelphia, he graduated from Lock Haven University with a degree in education after attending college on the GI Bill, payment for his service in the infantry in the European Theater in World War II. Aside from Nan and my Dad, no one had more influence in my life than Coach.

He taught social studies, and I had a particular love of civics, politics and history. It so happened that I had study halls during the same periods in the afternoon that he taught State and Local Government. I received permission several times to "audit" his class, to sit in for no credit and no grade, to simply be in his presence to soak up all I could.

He never stopped teaching or coaching.

The game clock was winding down and, as he had done so many times in his career, he called timeout.

He knew the score, assessed the situation and laid out the game plan.

The last timeout did not come in a packed gymnasium with his players huddled around him. This one came in his living room.

He leaned back in his chair, looked at me and said, matter-of-factly, "Who would have thought this is where we'd find ourselves?"

The hardest part of his days were the coughing spells each morning. But they only lasted 10 minutes, he said.

"I'm comfortable," he explained. "I'm in touch with the world. At my age, things like this can happen."

Thirty years earlier, he acknowledged, his reaction might have been different.

But this was now. And there was still time on the clock.

No chemotherapy, no radiation, no extraordinary measures. The cancer was beyond his control, and he accepted that.

What was within his grasp was his faith, and it was intact and unshakeable, just like the man I'd known since my youth.

He was at peace. The valley of the shadow of death was just another game situation.

Two weeks later, on Wednesday, John J. McNulty died quietly at his home in Brockway.

• • •

When he crested Smith's Hill east of Brockway for the first time in the late 1940s, Coach described a canopy of trees that enveloped Main Street. Many of them are long gone, but in their place another tree put down deep roots, spread out in all directions and towered above the landscape for more than 60 years.

When my parents divorced in 1972, Dad's path led to Denver and, later, to Omaha, Neb. Dad, who played ball for Coach in the mid-1950s, was and always is there for me and no father and son could possibly be closer. But when "there" was 1,000 or 1,500 miles away, it wasn't the same.

I remained in Brockway, on the cusp of my teenage years, with a big void that cried for a father figure.

Coach took me under his wing (at 6 feet, 6 inches tall, that's a LOT of wing) and, along with numerous other mentors, gave me the guidance I needed when I needed it most.

He salvaged me from the geekdom of those teen years and stayed with me through thick and thin all the years since.

There was a constituency that never quite grasped what Coach was about. His teaching methods were criticized, his coaching methods questioned.

He could have piled up a lot more wins in his 35-year coaching career if he'd taken the path of least resistance and played inferior competition. The quantity of wins didn't matter; he wanted quality wins, so his teams would be as prepared as they could be for the post-season, and the life that lay beyond.

Always looking ahead, always further ahead than the rest of us.

I just smiled, like the first member of an Agatha Christie book club to solve the mystery of "Ten Little Indians."

The "mystery" that shrouded the mountain that was the man was a figment of the beholders' imagination.

Character. Integrity. Honesty. And, lest I forget, uncompromising, too.

The one thing Coach never did was compromise his principles, sacrifice his integrity or dilute his values in order to accommodate others' flaws or excuse their failures.

He devoted his life to lifting us up ... family, friends, students, players ... to more than we thought we could be, more than the din of the madding crowd told us we were.

During one of our last chats, he bemoaned the disintegration of learning and the futility of "teaching to the test" that passes for education today. His occupation was "teacher," but his profession and his mission was "educator."

Life was one big learning laboratory, whether in his classroom or the gym, in the Legion home on Pershing Avenue, in Dick Gillung's pharmacy or in Coach's living room or back yard.

In school, some of us figured out that when he raised one arm and extended his index finger, he was ready to make a point. When both arms went up and both index fingers were extended, a revelation loomed.

In 2004, he was honored as Brockway's Sportsman of the Year at the annual athletic banquet. Getting him to the dinner that night involved a degree of planning and creative thinking that rivaled that of Operation Overlord, the Allied plan for the D-Day invasion of Europe in 1944.

He graciously accepted the homage and summed up his career as educator and coach by saying, "It was always about the kids." I shall ever be grateful for being one of his "kids."

He had to find it reassuring each morning to recognize the image in the bathroom mirror looking back at him. A lot of people can't make that claim. But Coach wasn't a lot of people. He was one of a kind, one of God's brightest lights in a vast universe that too often, too willingly succumbs to darkness and ignorance.

William Ernest Henley's "Invictus" capsulizes as well as any words I can find the man I call Coach, the friend I love, admire and respect.

Out of the night that covers me
black as the pit from pole to pole
I thank whatever gods may be
for my unconquerable soul

In the fell clutch of circumstance
I have not winced nor cried aloud
Under the bludgeonings of chance
my head is bloody, but unbowed

Beyond this place of wrath and tears
looms but the horror of the shade
and yet the menace of the years
finds, and shall find me, unafraid

It matters not how strait the gate
how charged with punishments the scroll
I am the master of my fate
I am the captain of my soul

Nick Hoffman

The Indefatigable

If Coach was the tip of the spear I'd carry into the battle of life, Harry Pinge was the shield I'd use to blunt the slings and arrows that would be hurled at me.

Many of the teachers and coaches I had in school were members of what would come to be called The Greatest Generation. They endured the Great Depression. They won World War II and saved civilization in the process.

Harry came from that mould. He was a U.S. Marine in the Pacific Theater. He taught health and physical education, and taught me a lot more than that.

The dictionary defines indefatigable as "incapable of being tired out; not yielding to fatigue; untiring."

That was Harry. In 30 years of column-writing, his name appeared in the subject line three times. To avoid redundancy, this is a composite version of all three.

A recent trip to Daydreamland took me back to high school gym class, of all places. Gym class? Never one of my strong suits. But there was one day . . .

One of the activities that we indulged in was "bleacher ball." That was baseball using a volleyball, hit with a closed fist, played in one-half of the gymnasium at dear, old Brockway High.

It was something that even a klutz like me had a fighting chance in, even though the "jocks" were very adept at fielding the ball and gunning down runners by throwing the ball at them, "burning" them.

The game was simple; hit the ball, run the bases, score. A ball hit onto the outfield bleachers freed the baserunners to go as far as they could. A ball that stuck at the top of the bleachers cleared the bases and was worth five or 10 extra runs. A ball that found its way through either of the two basketball hoops — one over second base, one in center field — cleared the bases and was worth 25 runs.

I routinely played catcher, a position where I could hide and minimize the damage to my teammates.

The official scorer and umpire was Harry Pinge, a legendary BAHS football and baseball coach and an all-around good guy. On this day, he was seated in the bleachers behind home plate. I came to bat, which I always dreaded. Nothing good could happen, only bad, worse and catastrophic.

I swung at a pitch and, glory be, sent the ball sailing toward center field. The backboard got in the way. The ball dropped through the basket. Dead center. The grandest slam of all.

I started my victory jog and looked up in the bleachers. There sat Mr. Pinge, flailing his arms and shouting as loud as he could, "Basket ball Basket ball!" He was more excited than I was.

I was still a klutz. Nothing ever did change that. But for one moment I was as good as anyone could be. Mr. Pinge knew that. And it pleased him. And me.

A few years later, when I became "legal," I'd shoot the breeze with Mr. Pinge over a few beers once in a while. By then, he had become "Harry."

His vocabulary contained some strange words, Tarawa and Saipan among them.

As I learned more about World War II, I understood

more about him. It's hard to imagine anyone who went through that seeing the world in the same way again.

But, since he'd seen the worst, maybe he appreciated the best a little bit more than the rest of us do.

Our paths don't cross as often as they once did, but I can still see him sitting in those bleachers with that twinkle in his eyes the day I hit that "Basket Ball," and the feeling of approval, coming from him, still means a great deal to me.

• • •

It was vintage Harry Pinge.

Having been named Brockway's Sportsman of the Year on Monday night (April 29, 2013) and given a standing ovation by the more than 300 on hand, the old coach stood silent for a moment while he collected his thoughts.

He'd just watched dozens of athletes receive plaques and a congratulatory handshake or hug from the guest speaker and women's professional basketball star Swin Cash.

His eyes aglow with their trademark twinkle, Harry noted the parade of "young people" just recognized and the hug many of them got from a "good looking lady." He got one, too.

A fixture in Brockway High School lore, Harry left a lasting impression over a 37-year teaching and coaching career that concluded in 1986.

In the 16 years since I wrote my first column about one of my mentors, the teacher and his pupil have grown closer. He's still teaching, and I'm still learning.

He endured a broken hip and some other complications last Fourth of July with the same indomitable spirit that has seen him through nearly nine decades of adventure. Harry just kept coming, relentlessly turning life's lemons into lemonade and sharing it with anyone who needed a sip.

As attendants maneuvered to load him onto a stretcher, knowing that any move no matter how slight would mean agony, the gritty Marine gritted his teeth and said something to the effect, "Let's get this done."

When Peter Varischetti introduced Harry as this year's honoree, he told the students, many of whom do not know or have not heard of Harry, that his life and his legacy enables them to enjoy the educational and athletic opportunities they have.

Fittingly, Swin Cash's remarks revolved around legacy and she challenged the students to give thought to how they want to be remembered some day.

I don't know if Harry ever looked in a mirror and asked himself about legacy, about what he could do to make a difference, to make the world a better, brighter place.

I rather doubt it; he was too busy being himself – husband, father, teacher, coach and friend, fighting a World War ... and making lemonade.

• • •

I have been blessed with a bushel of folks who shepherded me through my adolescent years, stood beside me in tough times later on and remained faithful friends ever since. That once swollen roster of mentors was reduced Wednesday with the passing of Harry Pinge.

Harry taught health and phys ed at Brockway for 37 years. My Dad – Class of 1955 - was one of his pupils, and baseball players. Harry, also a football coaching legend at Brockway, had a lasting impact on Dad's life, too. Our tears bridged the 1,000 miles between Brockway and Omaha when I called to give him the news.

Dad had moved west by the time I entered Harry's

universe in high school in the mid-1970s. The three of us stayed in touch through the years and Dad was particularly pleased when Harry was named Sportsman of the Year in Brockway last year.

I didn't play sports for Harry. But he "coached" me as if I did, steeling me for the game of life. Knowing Harry was in my corner, rooting for me was a source of inspiration and strength.

His wife Enes, son Mark and I were chatting about how times – and kids – have changed and of the drug epidemic that stalks them today. We ticked off a number of reasons for the disintegration and I added one more; "There aren't guys like him teaching them anymore."

For all the things life tossed his way that would have most men crying, Harry never forgot how to laugh, a hearty, throw-back-his-head burst accompanied by a smile from ear to ear.

When I was a junior in high school, I had to give a how-to demonstration to our speech class. It was spring and since I was playing varsity golf, I thought golf would be a good topic. After I finished swatting balls into a field across from the high school, the class headed back inside.

Harry was outside with one of his gym classes and asked what I was up to. He asked if I had a 4-wood, which I did. I handed him the steel-shafted, persimmon headed "baffy" and a ball. He rifled a shot across the road, a straight-as-a-string bullet that rose majestically, as if Arnold Palmer had socked it. Harry handed the club back. And smiled.

When Brockway honored him last year, I was glad to be able to say, "Thank you, Harry," one more time, because I'll never be able to say it enough.

During World War II, one song among many gave the troops hope that the dark days would pass. I can imagine Harry belting it out with some of his Marine comrades. I *can't sing it like Vera Lynn did, so I'll tap out the words on my keyboard, with accompaniment from Harry.*

We'll meet again,
Don't know where, don't know when,
But I know we'll meet again
Some sunny day.

Keep smilin' through
Just like you always do
Til the blue skies
Drive the dark clouds far away.

Indeed we will.

Style Matters;
Results Matter More

Mentors come in all sizes and shapes and leave their own distinct marks. One of them showed me that doing something right matters more than being loud about it.

Gary Keister, one of my Dad's boyhood chums and one of my mentors, died Monday at the age of 70.

The third floor and the back yard of the Hoffman household north of Brockway were havens for a gaggle of young men armed with imaginations as they grew up in the 1950s.

Two-man baseball was one of the staples, and Dad remembers Gary hitting his share of "homers" onto the railroad tracks in left field. While this and other pastimes afforded countless hours of enjoyment, the bonds of friendship were forged for life.

When I was in eighth grade, Gary was a business teacher and the golf coach at Brockway Area High School. His wife, Irene, was a guidance counselor and another of my tutors and boosters.

By the time I was able to join the team as a freshman, Gary had relinquished the coaching duties to Bob Cherubini, now the elementary school principal at Brockway. Both of them encouraged me to work hard and stay with it. I did, and learned a lot about life in the bargain.

Gary was a borough councilman while I was in high school and he nurtured my passion for politics as well. Somewhere in my house, there's a black T-shirt with white lettering that says "Senator," a gift from Gary for my help with a traffic survey.

Senator? Yes, my first long-term goal in life (as a fifth-grader) was to be president of the U.S., but I backed off that and decided that being a U.S. Senator would suffice.

My classmates and I were lucky to have had so many teachers who concentrated more on opening our minds than our textbooks.

Gary's career turned toward the administrative end and he did stints as both assistant principal and principal at Dear Old Brockway High, in the days when schools were a whole lot more than locked-down day care centers.

Off the golf course, Gary met the challenge of reining in my often unbridled enthusiasm for causes and issues.

During the 1970s edition of the energy crisis, I remember bantering about the need for a windfall profits oil tax, having heard President Carter propose such a thing.

"What, exactly," he asked me one day in the cafeteria, "is that, Nicholas?"

"Uhhhhh ... well, I don't know exactly," I sheepishly replied.

Lesson learned.

Gary was such an easygoing and disarming man that it wasn't always easy to see him as an administrator, contrasted with the loud, confrontational, sometimes dictatorial style we too often see exhibited by those who hold those jobs.

But as I watched, I saw a man who could set aside any personal need to "win" in order to do the right thing. He preferred to reach consensus rather than the boiling point.

So do I, and Gary is one of the people who had a great deal to do with "inculcating" (one of his pet words) me with that approach.

He got things done, maybe not as quickly as some would have preferred, but far more often than not the things he got done were done right.

We share our walk through life with a cast of countless fellow travelers, some for decades, others for a short while. Some of them leave their mark, some of them we call "friend." Gary Keister will always be one of the good guys.

Counter Intelligence

E ducation is where you find it.

Sometimes, it takes place in the back seat of a car on a secluded dirt road, or while you and your buddies warm yourselves around a fire next to a 16-gallon keg, or while you're doing something else you've been told not to do which only makes you want to do it more.

Much more likely in my case, the extra credit work took place at the local diner on the way to school.

When I was a kid, not all of my education took place in the hallowed halls of the Brockway Area High School.

I often got an early start on the way to school by stopping at the old E&E Restaurant on Main Street.

All manner of colorful characters frequented the E&E every morning, where they drank coffee and, as time allowed, solved problems great and small.

To the uninitiated, it may have seemed the seat of borough government was the restaurant, not the borough building a block over.

On Monday, the most colorful of those characters, Jiggs DeSantis Sr., died.

Jiggs was a character in the best sense of the word. His reputation preceded him and depending on whom you listened to, he was either the biggest rabble-rouser in town or Moses without the robe, sandals and tablets.

He was actually a little bit of both.

I recall the anticipation that preceded the first time I ever met him. All I knew about him is what I heard, including his storied tirades directed at borough government, about how this could be done better, this not at all.

His son, John (Jiggs Jr.), was a year ahead of me in school and I spent a good deal of time as the football team's trainer attending to his various battlefield wounds.

Since I had to walk past the DeSantis home on the corner of Second Avenue and Alexander Street on my way to and from school each day, Jiggs, Sr. or Jr., became a part of everyday life.

Those sessions at the E&E were eye-openers.

Anything and anybody was fair game, from the state of affairs at city hall, which was always under siege for something - which streets were being paved, what the police were up to - to why the football team couldn't run the ball effectively or why the basketball team couldn't break a man-to-man press.

Lots of questions, lots of answers and, as it turned out, few solutions.

Jiggs had an opinion about everything and he wasn't bashful about expressing his thoughts. That's what made him uniquely Jiggs.

Right or wrong, and I'd say he probably batted around .500, he was one of my boyhood mentors. Some of the others didn't care for him and he didn't care for some of them. But I never had to choose between them, because they all stood on their own, based on what they meant to me, not to someone else.

To sit and listen to Jiggs and the other E&E cast debate and argue was a privilege, a free (except for the coffee, which was 53 cents a cup, with a refill, if memory serves me right), inside look at what being a grown-up was supposedly all about.

I looked for the "secrets" of their success.

There weren't any.

I looked for those who had life "figured out," so I could be a "winner," too.

No such magic.

I looked for heroes without flaws, who knew it all and took on all comers.

I never found them, no matter where or how hard I looked.

What I did find were friends who allowed me to walk along with them, who shared their opinions and outlooks and, indirectly, encouraged me to find my own. Along the way, I began to realize that growing older and growing up weren't the same thing.

Time passed, we both grew older, and Jiggs and I saw less of each other. When we did run into one another, I kiddingly implored him to "behave himself" and not embarrass himself or his wonderful wife Cora with his antics. He would laugh and nod, but an ever-present and mischievous twinkle in his eyes betrayed the kid in him, trapped in an adult body, and he always left me wondering what he'd be up to next.

No that it mattered.

I already knew all I needed or wanted to know.

He was my friend.

One I'll miss.

One I'll always cherish.

Window To The World

At the other end of town, the East End, was another institution of higher learning that I was compelled to attend from time to time.

I spent part of Sunday afternoon standing in line at the Carlson Funeral Home in Brockway to pay respects to the late Gene Ross, who died Thursday.

Gene was a barber by trade and he, along with Beano Donati and Bill Anderson, took turns cutting my hair for the first 20-plus years of my life.

Barbershops held a mystical attraction for me aside from the need to be shorn on a regular basis. Mom and Dad paid for that.

The rest, eavesdropping on "grown-up" stuff while it was discussed, argued, debated and resolved, was free.

At Gene's, the barber's chair was positioned so he could whirl customers around and give them a view through the large picture window at the front of the shop, onto and across Main Street, where the late Steve and Margaret Rendos lived and, next door, my Aunt Helen Repiscak's home, at the corner of McCain Street.

There were three or four chairs arrayed around a table full of magazines and newspapers to browse through. My newspaper interest was enhanced by Gene and the Pittsburgh Post-Gazette that graced his shop and John

McNulty's newspaper habit as a high school basketball coach. I guess it rubbed off.

What I didn't appreciate as a youngster sitting in that barbershop was the broader view through that window. It was more than just Main Street in Brockway and, as I grew older, I began to appreciate that.

I looked around Sunday afternoon and saw numerous World War II veterans waiting in line, in front of and behind me. Another of their comrades had fallen and they came to say good-bye.

Their view of life was probably much the same as Gene's, I imagine. Born in the late 'Teens and early 1920s, they were just "kids" when the Great Depression uprooted their way of life. Just as they and the nation struggled through that calamity and began to emerge, WWII came along and delivered a second punch. Gene served in the Army, a member of the 85th Battalion 10th Mountain Division of Rangers.

To Gene's generation's everlasting credit, neither the Depression nor the war delivered a knockout. Either one could have; both probably should have.

The Rev. Robert Schuller says it like this: "Tough times don't last; tough people do." That generation proved it.

As the 1900s ended, an author said that generation, Gene's generation, saved the world and enabled us to celebrate a new millennium.

Life after the war wasn't especially easy, either, as physical afflictions brought new and increasing pains on Gene.

But he endured. I don't think there's a person in town who can say he ever saw Gene without a smile on his face.

That's the way he was. That's they way they were.

I should have gone up and down that line at the funeral

home Sunday and said "Thank you" to every one of those veterans.

Imagine, if you can, where we'd be if men and women of that era, like Gene, hadn't endured so bravely and sacrificed so freely.

Words of praise will soon echo at memorials and in cemeteries on Memorial Day. But if some enterprising school administrator is looking for a new nine-week course for senior high students, he could do worse than to create something that puts young people in coffee shops and barbershops or anywhere else those men and women are so that some of their grace and strength can rub off.

Assessment tests can measure how well the kids know "who, what, when and where" but it takes more than that, much more, to pass life's "final."

It takes what Gene and his generation had - and gave so freely - so that I can sit at a home computer in my bedroom and write these words.

I hope someone remembers them because, some day - maybe even today - we'll need their grit.

And that, as I look back, was the much broader view of life that could be seen through Gene's window.

The Quiet Man

Occasionally, when I walked by the American Legion home on Pershing Avenue on my way home, I'd stop and pay a visit, especially if John McNulty's red station wagon was there, which it often was.

It seems like the people who make the biggest differences make the least noise going about it. One of Coach's best friends, and one of the men I most admired growing up, spent a lot of time at the Legion, too.

One of the unique aspects of life in a small town is how the words and deeds of one very special man can have a positive and enduring impact on everyone he comes in contact with.

In Bedford Falls in It's a Wonderful Life, it was George Bailey. In Brockway, it was Ed Biss, who passed away Friday.

Anyone who knows anything about Brockway knows of the life and legacy of this kind, gentle, humble man. While he earned his living at Brockway Clay Co., he made his mark through many other endeavors.

If it wasn't for Ed Biss's imagination, Brockway High School's sports teams could well be the Lions, Lambs or Bulldogs. But we're Rovers because, way back when, the football team didn't have a field to call its own. The team "roved" the countryside, playing its games on the road.

Then-sportswriter Ed Biss coined the term "Rovers." It stuck.

Ed Biss's impact on the community he called home was far more profound than just a moniker for the high school sports teams. Everywhere he went and everything he touched was better because of him.

A member of the Brockway School Board for 24 years in the years following World War II, Ed Biss was known to have reached into his own pocket to pay for equipment that was beyond the board's budget.

When Little League baseball arrived in town circa 1950, Ed Biss was one of its founding fathers and he remained one of its benefactors to the day he died. Ditto Legion Baseball.

His works extended to his country — a World War II veteran who counted five Bronze Stars among his decorations and was the heart and soul of Parson-Marnati Post 95 of the American Legion, where he served as commander, finance officer and service officer and authored the award-winning Willie and Joe newsletter for more than three decades. The American Legion honored him in 1987 with its highest award — The Distinguished Service Medal. He was devoted to his church, to the community, to its youth and to anyone in need.

He annually presented the Edward and Evelyn Biss nursing scholarship and the American Legion Citizenship Award to Brockway High seniors.

It wasn't only what Ed Biss did in his remarkable 82 years of life. It's how he did it — quietly, without expectation of reward or recognition. He did everything because it was the honorable, decent and right thing to do.

When Brockway honored Ed Biss with a testimonial dinner in 1970, Msgr. Paul Gooder said, "Ed . . . the man stands for sincerity, integrity, humility, tolerance, the *wisdom to make the right decision and charity. How many people do we find who give of themselves as Ed Biss has?"*

In 1985, when the Brockway Sports Boosters Club honored Biss, John McNulty said, "If someone were to ask me 'What is goodness, humility, kindness, compassion, love and charity?', my answer would be Ed Biss."

As long as the Rovers play ball, as long as Little League bats crack, as long as Memorial Day, Veterans Day and the Fourth of July call us to remember how lucky we are and why, as long as duty to country and to fellow man mean anything, the legacy of Ed Biss will be secure, cherished by those fortunate enough to have known him and called him friend.

The Right Prescription

My education wasn't limited to daylight hours, either. By night, it wasn't unusual for my studies to end up in the back room of Gillung's Pharmacy. Thinking back, Dick must have been the first subject of my reflective columns. He died in 1988, while I was the bureau manager of the newspaper's Brookville office.

I was deeply saddened to learn last week of the death of Dick Gillung, longtime Brockway pharmacist and a close friend for many years.

Dick had a keen mind as well as a full measure of practical common sense, packaged in a robust, often wry sense of humor and wrapped in the aroma of an omnipresent cigar.

He had the ability to sift through complex issues or dismantle a tough question and pull up all the opposing points of view, to play "devil's advocate," in other words and keep things in perspective.

We spent many, many long hours in the back room of Dick's drug store, watching television and sipping coffee and, more often than not, proffering our solutions to the woes of mankind.

Dick earned my undying respect when he dutifully cared for and nursed his ailing mother for a number of years until her passing two years ago.

Duty was a cornerstone of Dick's life and he carried out his duties – some pleasant, many not – faithfully.

He knew what was right and what was wrong and he had a way of making "duty" and "obligation" and "commitment" understandable to many a starry-eyed youth, including me.

Growing up can be a pretty confusing, often frightening experience. Dick saw through the façade that most kids – again, including me – put up at one time or another – that they (we, me) have all the answers.

Dick knew there were questions, too; a lot more questions than answers; questions that were tough to ask and often tougher to answer (some even to this day).

But many a young man in Brockway graduated from Dick's "backroom school" with a broader and more realistic view of life.

Few if any of the solutions that we concocted for the world's ills in Dick's back room ever made it off of our drawing board.

What did emerge was at least one young man who will always be grateful for the time Dick took to put a different – often fresher – face on life.

He occupied a very small corner of the world for an all-too-short period of time. But he put into life so much more than he took from it, and he'll be missed very, very much.

But never forgotten.

Nick Hoffman

A Bittersweet Chapter In Life's Plan

It seemed like everywhere I went and everyone I met had a life lesson for me. And I soaked it up. Maybe it was my insatiable curiosity. Maybe it was a subconscious search for father figures. Maybe it was a little bit of both. Whatever it was, I loved it.

Then, suddenly, it was over. Ready or not, it was time to move on.

Billy Joel's song, "We Didn't Start the Fire" from 1989 hit some of the highlights of the '70s, although it left out leisure suits, bell bottoms and platform heels. The ones he did include are highlighted below (cutting out the late '60s and the '80s would have ruined the beat, and no child of the '70s would ever allow that to happen ☺

Birth control, Ho Chi Minh, Richard Nixon back again
*Moonshot, Woodstock, **Watergate, punk rock***
Begin, Reagan, Palestine, Terror on the airline
Ayatollahs in Iran, Russians in Afghanistan
Wheel of Fortune, Sally Ride, heavy metal, suicide
Foreign debts, homeless Vets, AIDS, Crack, Bernie Goetz
Hypodermics on the shores, China's under martial law
Rock and Roller Cola wars, I can't take it anymore

My senior year was my best year, a climax long in the making. The principal tried to talk me into skipping it and going to Clarion State College, to get a head start on college.

I had become something of a thorn in his side. I went to school board meetings and had the audacity to report back to the students on some of the decisions that affected us. That resulted in a threat to expel me for "inciting the students to riot."

But things worked out. I stayed and had the time of my life. I had emerged from my burrow into the sunlight of life, made friends and formed relationships that would last a lifetime.

The assistant principal, Ray Doolittle, wrote in my yearbook, *"Good luck Nick. Of all the students who have attended BAHS, I feel that you have progressed and matured as much or more than any other student I can think of. I sincerely wish you the very best."*

That meant a lot then, and still does.

But before the first day of the rest of my life, there was graduation night. Oh, what a night!

The Class of 1979, 90 of us adorned in our caps and gowns seated on the stage in the auditorium at dear old Brockway High.

There were four speakers, and I was in the anchor spot.

Nan and Papa were there. So was Mom. And Bubba. And Wee Wee and his wife, Auntie Rose. It would have been nice if Dad could have been there, but I understood. I'd have to tell him about it.

In my speech, I talked about how our lives would be measured. "Did I make this world a better place?, "Did I bring happiness or hope to someone?", "Was I there when someone needed me?" and "Whether I lost or won, did I fight the good fight and remain true to my ideals?"

I concluded by sharing a poem Dad wrote for me when I turned 16. *"I would like to think, however, that my father wrote this poem not for me alone, but for every young person in this land that has a dream,"* I said. *"If there were nothing else in my life to guide me through, this poem would be more than amply sufficient."*

"A 16th birthday is quite a time, and I'm going to write this little rhyme

"To let you know though I'm away, my thoughts are with you on this day.

"Of all the birthdays that you've had, this one makes me kind of sad.

"It's a bittersweet chapter in life's plan that changes you from boy to man."

As often as I'd practiced, that was the line that started choking me up. *"Bittersweet chapter ... boy to man."*

I looked up, back to a corner of the auditorium. Coach McNulty was standing there, and next to him was ... I squinted ... Dad!

Nan and Papa paid for his flight home to be there with me. I should have figured it out earlier that day. One of Dad's bowling buddies stopped at the house, where I was reclining on a swing. "Did your Dad make it in?" he asked. I said no, and wondered where Dean had gotten such a notion.

The fear that I'd be able to finish the speech after realizing Dad was there was a very present one. How could I get through this? I'm sure Nan's lips were whispering in God's ear, asking him to give me strength. He did.

With tears streaming down my face, my voice choked

with emotion, I kept going, even though the next line was another tough one.

"And you'll find as years go by, my son, that your boyhood days were lots of fun.

"But the sands of time run very fast and the joys of youth are too soon past.

"You'll find the real tests in your life begin when you choose career and wife.

"And these choices will soon be yours to face; you'll have to go and find your place.

"There's lots of advice I'd like to share but I find it hard since I'm not there.

"So I'll sum it up in this small way and hope you'll heed what I have to say.

"Since this life of yours will rush away, you should make good use of every day.

"Think long and wise before you choose and stay away from drugs and booze.

"Work hard, play hard and get your rest, and always thank God that you've been blessed

"With talent and wisdom that can make you great, and if that's your wish, don't sit and wait.

"Go forth and do your thing young man and as you go believe you can.

"But if you fail you must not cry; at least you gave your dreams a try.

"And whether you find success or not, make sure you give it all you've got

"No matter then, if you lost or won, I'll always be proud to call you son."

There wasn't a dry eye in the house. I wept like a baby. My best friend Jim was seated front and center, crying. Two of my classmates, Jeanne Cooper and Jill

Holding, scolded me for breaking my promise not to make them cry.

It was a magical night. Those tears washed away a lot of torment. I never could have imagined that things would turn out like this. And I didn't fully comprehend how many people had a hand in it.

School Days, School Daze

Dad was right about many things in that poem and the first one I discovered was just how fast the "sands of time" run and how this life does rush away.

I enrolled at Penn State, which used a trimester system in those days. I spent the first seven terms at Penn State DuBois, which allowed me to live at home (and save some money). That meant I didn't lose complete touch with the teachers who were such a big part of my life. I thought about them frequently, and still do. The impending retirement of one of them in the early 1990s took me on a trip down memory lane.

As another school year comes to a close, I find myself thinking about school days, about the people, places and things that defined that time of life and made it special.

One by one, many of the teachers who defined those days, who breathed life and substance and excitement into learning are or have retired.

One of them stopped by the golf course in Brockway last weekend. With my tongue firmly in cheek, I asked Mrs. Siple, "How many days?" Sensing the unspoken "rest" of the question, she somewhat gleefully said, "Four more days forever."

At the end of this week, Mrs. Siple will close out a distinguished career at Brockway Area High School. Who will teach the students about the Aswan High Dam in Egypt, I wondered. Memories began flooding back. As I daydreamed, those distant high school days suddenly and perceptibly seemed much closer in time and space than the 14 years that have passed since they played out.

Bonnie Siple, John McNulty, Jim Hale, Bert Riggle, Ray and Alberta Doolittle, Charlie Zoffuto, Harry Pinge, Gary and Irene Keister, Caroline Longwell — the list goes on. There are still a few teachers I know at dear old Brockway High — Mr. Foulkrod, Mr. Schuckers, Mr. and Mrs. Ball and Mr. and Mrs. Sprague, to name a few.

The last time I saw Mr. Ball, he asked a "Remember when . . ." question. I did remember. And I snickered to myself. Mr. Schuckers just won't let me forget my adventures on the senior class trip to Florida.

Even with some of the "old guard" still in place in the palace, it will be increasingly difficult to visit the old stomping grounds with so many of the "mainstays" gone. They played a larger-than-life role in my growing up. They didn't indoctrinate. Or preach. Or coerce. They taught by stimulating and challenging the mind, not by reprogramming it. And in doing so they made so much of the world become more understandable.

I remember giving up study halls to sit in on John McNulty's state and local government class. I so enjoyed being in coach's presence, of being challenged to ask "why" instead of "what," to question the established order of things instead of accepting it at face value, of learning about life and things that matter much by some means other than rote recitation using spoon-fed facts. So many of my classmates never could understand that.

The nightmares of algebra and geometry spring to mind. No matter how hard I tried, Mr. Riggle and Mr. Sprague couldn't convey to me why algebra mattered much.

I just couldn't grasp the concept of doing mathematical calculations using letters. I never quit trying and they never quit teaching and Mr. Sprague told me once that the only reason I passed his classes was because I didn't quit trying. In doing so, he taught me something far more valuable than $(x + y)(x + y) = x2 + 2xy + y2$ ... or something like that. ☺

Little did I know that diagramming sentences on the blackboard in Mrs. Sprague's English class would prepare me, in no small way, for what I do to make my living — breaking down copy and turning it into comprehensible prose.

My love affair with the weather maps in Mrs. Doolittle's science class continues to this day. I missed the "birds and the bees" movie in Mr. Hale's biology class that everyone looked forward to, but I still recall the bleacher ball basket shot I made in Mr. Pinge's gym class. Scored 25 "runs" with that shot and was a gym class jock for 5 minutes.

The confrontations in the principal's office with Superintendent Jim Manners remain fresh in my mind but the man I once regarded as an adversary is now a respected friend.

One by one, they are retiring or have retired. Some have passed on. But the more time that passes, the fonder the memories become. Those memories are of a much simpler time, even though it seemed pretty complicated, hectic and puzzling back then. Somehow, though, I sensed that it was special, even then, and I soaked up as much of it as I could.

Oh, but for a spoonful of that youthful innocence and idealism now. If only the hands of time would turn back and allow me a few more minutes in their presence, one more look at the world through the eyes of a teenager with great expectations.

Nick Hoffman

Yes, Mrs. Siple, four more days forever for a career, perhaps, but to you and to all those whose classrooms I was privileged to sit in, whose mettle I was allowed to test and whose pupil I was fortunate to have been, an eternity of gratitude and good wishes.

Play Away, Please

Being part of the football and basketball teams was important because it drew me out of my shell, even though I didn't appreciate how much that mattered until years later.

What I did understand from early on was how much I loved the game of golf. In all the years since, nothing has consumed me like golf. Dad started golfing when he worked at the "lab" at Brockway Glass for Dr. Jim Poole, an expert in the science behind making glass containers.

So it was only natural that during the summer of 1973 while I was visiting in Denver, Dad introduced me to the game, one that I grew to love and one that taught me a lot about myself.

There are a handful of high holy days in my golfing world. Sunday was one of them: the final round of the U.S. Open.

It's hard for a golfer to watch that pageant of torture and triumph without putting oneself in the player's place. What would I do if that was me in Payne's or Phil's or Tiger's place?

Nick Hoffman

It must be natural to think like that, with so many players recounting tales of their childhood, practicing on the putting green until dark, imagining that "If he makes this devilish 6-inch putt, Nick Hoffman will be the U.S. Open champ."

I still do that when I practice but two things have changed. I'm a lot older and the putts are a lot tougher.

I was on the practice putting green at Scottish Heights Monday morning when I was, quite unexpectedly, whisked back nearly a quarter of a century.

A young boy, maybe 10 or 11, headed to the 1st tee. He wore glasses, shorts and a T-shirt and had his golf bag slung over his shoulder. He was by himself. He belted his tee shot into the right rough, gouged his second shot to the left side of the fairway, then hit it again toward the green.

• • •

As I watched, I remembered when I was about his age and my Grandma drove me to the course at 8 a.m. for one of those marathon days - 36 holes, sometimes as many as 54 - often alone, just me and my flat, loopy swing against the course.

Some days I'd get so disgusted that I'd quit in mid-round and walk home, following the railroad tracks to my house and swearing that I'd never play that stupid game again. Within an hour or so, I'd cool off, figure out what I was doing wrong and ask Grandma for a ride back to the course. She always obliged.

Then, after it was too dark to play any more, I'd stumble back down the tracks and begin preparing for tomorrow.

I still don't know why I persisted. There was near-unanimous agreement that I had no talent for the game. Even my Dad told me that years later, saying he only wanted to introduce me to the game when we played the par 3 Centennial course near Denver. I shot 68. Par was 27.

I didn't have a set of clubs, so Dad lent me his since he wasn't playing much in those days.

I didn't have the $20 for a student membership at

Brockway Glass Golf Course, so I borrowed it from my grandparents.

And I didn't have any reason to keep going round and round and round that course.

I shot 81 for 9 holes when I finally got all 9 holes in without losing all the balls I had with me. That didn't count penalty strokes, which I didn't know about. I thought those white stakes were decorations or something.

Golf balls were cheap by today's standards but I couldn't afford Titleists. It was Club Specials or Spalding Eagles at $2 or $3 a sleeve; one ball costs that or more today.

There was always the Green Stamp option, though. The S&H Green Stamp store in DuBois had Lee Trevino signature Dunlop balls and, if I didn't have the money for balls at Perk Binney's Pro Shop, Grandma and I would paste in the Green Stamps and go to DuBois to get some more ammunition.

Pop (usually cherry) and Reese's Cups were the staple diet that kept me going.

They talk about the pressure that players face in the U.S. Open.

It pales in comparison to the pressure that led to the worst choke job I ever pulled.

It was a Saturday evening and I was wrapping up another marathon. I was getting better but still hadn't broken 60 for 9 holes. That night, I had 48 for 8 holes. I was playing alone and, as I walked to the 9th tee, wondered if anyone would believe me when I announced that I had finally broken 60. Then I reminded myself that I hadn't yet.

And I didn't.

I forget the gory details but I took a 12 for a nice, round 60. It's a tough hole, but not that tough. I choked. I wondered if I'd ever get any better. God, that hurt.

But I was back the next day, and the next and the next, rarin' to go.

I eventually did break 60. Made the high school team at Brockway. And the college team at Penn State DuBois. Won a trophy or two. Met some of the best people I've ever known. Made some of the best friends I'll ever have. Had some of the times of my life.

• • •

Back to Monday morning. I hit a couple more putts, looked up and saw the young man headed down the hill on the 2ⁿᵈ hole. When I left the course to go to work, he was on his way to the 5ᵗʰ tee, looking a bit perplexed but determined. I waved - to him and to days long ago that were as satisfying as any I have ever known. Or ever will.

I hope they're as good to him.

I don't remember thinking much about how my family compared to my classmates when it came to money. I knew we didn't have a lot, but I had a roof over my head, decent clothes and food in the fridge.

Rather than pout about those who had more than I did, I had sympathy for those who didn't have as much. And most of us were so busy enjoying what we did have, we weren't bothered by what we didn't. Perspective means a lot.

I went out for the golf team in 1976, my freshman year. Golf was played in the spring then, which meant dealing with less than ideal conditions. As often as not, it was cold and wet and miserable. But like most of the rest of the guys, as soon as we saw patches of green on the course, out we went. Until that happened, we spent time in the gym at North Street Elementary hitting plastic balls off turf mats or learning The Rules of Golf on an overhead projector.

Coach Bob Cherubini knew, like everyone else except me, that I didn't have what it took. But he "humored" me.

There was a practice green at the far end of the

Brockway Glass Golf Course, between the 6th green and 7th tee. There was enough space around that green to make up several teeing areas so that I had my own private pitch and putt course – 20- to 30-yard shots. It kept me busy and, more important, far enough away from everyone else that I couldn't hurt anyone. I didn't mind. I became a pretty decent chipper and putter and as most golfers will attest, that's where strokes are made or lost.

"What do I have to do to play with the rest of the team?" I asked Bob.

We made a deal. The 1st hole at Brockway going out paralleled the 9th hole coming in. Both were par 4s; the 1st wasn't particularly hard but the 9th was a challenge.

Play those two holes in less than 20 strokes and I could play with "the big boys." That wouldn't be much of a challenge for anyone with a little bit of game. But to me, Bob may as well have asked me to climb Mt. Everest.

I suppose a lot of guys in my situation would've bristled at being put through hoops like that. I didn't care. I wanted to play golf.

I knew what I had to do. It took a while, but I did it and gleefully reported back to Bob. My work had paid off.

Until I saw it on video, I presumed my swing looked like Jack Nicklaus's or any other golfer's. Not quite. I was more like Dr. Victor Frankenstein, building his monster piece by piece. I took - and still take – the club very much inside as I start the backswing, then hoist it up to shoulder level and "loop" as I return the clubface back to impact. If you've seen Jim Furyk's swing, you have an idea what mine looks like.

It isn't pretty, but it works. I know folks with great looking swings who can't break 100. Unique as it is, my swing repeats and I understand it. That it works is more important than how it looks.

I was the number one golfer on the varsity team in my senior year and lost only one match. I was in the top 10 at the District Championship; shot 81 with five three-putts. At Penn State DuBois, I received the Coach's Award in 1979 and was MVP in 1980.

I won three straight Championship Flight titles at Brockway Glass from 1983-85. I added a fourth in 1994. Two of those first three were contested over 36 holes of match play in which I managed to defeat Dave Genevro, which was no easy task. Dave was a year ahead of me in school and was top dog in his senior year, the guy to beat. We became – and remain – best friends. Frankly, I idolized him. Dave inspired me, and to be able to play at the same level as he did meant the world to me.

I'm glad I stuck around and answered the question: "What do I have to do to play with the rest of the team?"

I could have found something else to do. Instead, I added the golf course to the list of places where I learned more about life and myself than any book or classroom could have taught me.

Golf was a big part of my growing up. I worked harder than most because I had to. I was willing to pay that price. I made a lot of friends and had a lot of fun. No matter what my handicap was, I would have kept playing just for the camaraderie, of being part of something.

I don't play as much today as I used to or wish I could, but when I wipe the dust off the clubs, I'm just as likely to go to the driving range as I am the 1st tee. I love to practice. It didn't make perfect in my case, but it sure did make it better.

No matter how much I learned about the history of the game, course layout, agronomy and running a pro shop, I learned a lot more about myself. That's a big deal in anyone's life.

Leave 'Em Laughing When You Go

When you're on the course and having one of those days when you have no idea where the next shot is going – only that it won't be someplace good – it's difficult to remember that golf is a **game** that is supposed to be **fun**.

Arnold Gustav Becker – "AG" for short – made it fun for whoever he was playing with even if he wasn't having a good day.

It isn't always easy to laugh, especially these days. Times are tough, winter is closing in quicker than we'd like and the Steelers haven't hit their stride yet (although the Chargers might disagree).

When I received word Sunday afternoon that Arnold G. "AG" Becker of Brockway had died, my sadness at hearing the news from his son Mark, one of my longtime best friends, was tempered by a smile when I thought of AG and his wit.

Mr. Becker, a native of Wisconsin, was the retired vice president of industrial relations and human resources at Brockway Glass, before it merged with Owens-Illinois more than 20 years ago. Labor peace was one of the hallmarks that enabled Brockway Glass, and the community it called home, to prosper for generations. AG was one of the peacekeepers.

I thought about him a couple weeks ago when DeVere Sheesley, former president and CEO of Brockway Glass, died in Florida at the age of 99. By my reckoning, that left AG alone among his contemporaries of a bygone age that saw a little glass manufacturer grow and mature to become the second largest glass container maker on planet Earth.

It is fitting that AG outlasted Sheesley and Jack McMackin, Finley Hess and Glenn Mengle and Bob Warren and others from those halcyon days in Glasstown because AG was in a class by himself.

He was a straight-to-the-point, matter-of-fact man in his public persona, borne no doubt of the necessity of dealing with the responsibilities of his job.

But "off camera," AG was a fun-loving and funny man. Many people are capable of humor. AG had wit, a droll sense of humor that was as sophisticated as it was sharp. Leno and Letterman had nothing on him when it came to lighting up a room, and I think AG would have been just as comfortable as a stand-up comic as he was in the role of a captain of industry.

He and his wife Marilyn raised five children: sons Bruce, Kurt, Mark and Craig and daughter Wendy. Between his duties at Brockway Glass and their duties as parents, Marilyn was instrumental in breathing life into the Brockway Area Ambulance Service while AG found time to serve as a Brockway Borough councilman and contribute significantly to many other community efforts.

He also found time to enjoy the game of golf, and those who shared a round with him counted it a blessing, often left in the dust of his cart as he raced to the next shot, and in stitches by the rapier-like wit that bore AG's trademark.

A long and busy life, punctuated by love and laughter, came to an end after nearly 90 years.

But as I pointed out to Mark when we talked Sunday, his father's legacy includes Owens-Brockway Glass's ongoing operations in the Tri-County Area that now include three glass factories and a machine shop that enable nearly 1,000 employees and numerous vendors and suppliers to make a living and provide for their families.

Whether negotiating a contract, outrunning fellow competitors in a golf cart or walking his dog along Main Street in the early morning (and cleaning up after it), AG Becker lived and loved and laughed, and left us, if no longer laughing uproariously with him, at least smiling at the thought of him.

His Honor; My Pleasure

I spent a lot of time at the golf course, playing and, for 10 years, partnering with course Superintendent Jim Beimel to run the pro shop operation.

Between the course and the pro shop, I met a lot of very good people, including one man I couldn't help but admire ... and love.

Roger Burkett, a kid at heart gift-wrapped in a 91-year-old body and one of the shining stars and guiding lights in my life, died Sunday.

It's impossible to explain Roger; he had to be experienced.

He had a long and distinguished career at Brockway Glass, where he served as both a plant manager and area plants manager.

He was also one of the driving forces behind what is now the Owens-Brockway Golf Course, which started as a 3-hole layout in 1954. It was at that venue that our friendship flourished.

Roger had a zest for life that was uniquely his. He had an unquenchable thirst for information, absorbing everything he could like a sponge. We spent countless hours in the pro shop drinking coffee and discussing the affairs of the day.

Politics was a special favorite and we painstakingly

examined the political scene, talking about shows he'd watched or stories he'd read.

Roger gave me insight into his career at Brockway Glass, a behind the scenes look into the company's heyday and of how, to be successful, it was more important to manage people than to operate machinery.

And Roger surely loved people. And I dearly loved him.

Golf was an abiding passion and he loved to go "hit the ball." He hopped aboard the technology express and, well into his 80s, was tinkering with the latest innovations, striving for those few extra yards that all golfers crave.

And he loved to watch "the boys" play. He'd stake out a position on the course - the 5th tee and behind the 9th green were favorites - and watch us make our way through our ritual skins games, seeking explanations for shots missed and enjoying, as much or more than we, the good shots.

A few years ago, we played a season-ending tournament on a rainy Sunday in cold, raw, soaking wet conditions that nobody should have been playing in. But Roger was right there with us, hitting every shot, trying to contribute, enjoying the hunt, oblivious to the foul conditions. When the event was shortened to 9 holes, Roger wondered why; there was more golf to play, wasn't there?

At a late season scramble at Pinecrest Country Club in Brookville, Roger came along for the ride, literally, as our cheerleader and gallery. Having him there made us all determined to play a little harder.

He and I played one morning at Brockway. There's a pond in front of the 3rd tee and, depending on where the markers were, Roger would play left or right around the pond. On this day, the markers were right, which meant Roger had to play up the adjoining 5th fairway. His drive rattled around in a cluster of trees bordering the pond, which meant I'd drive him up that route to his ball.

As I put my driver back in my bag, I looked around and saw Roger, on foot, already in hot pursuit of his drive, anxious to catch up to it and hit it again.

"C'mon, Roger. I'll take you over to it," I said. But it was too late. Off he went to hit it, find it, and hit it again. I saw him again 300 yards later, still chasing it and hitting it.

His optimism and zeal were infectious.

One story above all about Roger capsulizes the man I knew and adored.

One morning, on the first tee at Brockway, he and I were ready to go. He had the honor.

He put a tee into the ground and reached to put the ball on it. Roger had a touch of Parkinson's and his trembling hand made it hard for him to set the ball atop that peg.

The ball fell off.

Roger picked it up.

It fell off again.

Resisting the urge to do it for him for fear of insulting him, I watched as my friend struggled mightily before finally managing to tee that ball.

Then, straightening up and sighing but with his trademark twinkle in his eye, he said, "That's the tough part."

Always in search of better, taking nothing for granted, embracing life and enjoying every minute of it. That was Roger.

When we last talked "in depth" in October, we knew that things were changing. Resolute, with a tear in his eye, he assured me that he wasn't afraid of whatever was ahead.

And I knew that was so.

No one who embraced life like Roger Burkett had any room for fear.

Quiet In The Ranks

Helping to manage the golf course put me in touch with a lot of quality people, not the least of which was a retired U.S. Army colonel.

A colorful, ebullient and devoted Brockway resident died Saturday.

Bernard L. Garred Jr., retired U.S. Army lieutenant colonel, kept life interesting for me in the 20-odd years I knew him.

The Colonel embodied devotion and dedication, qualities that surely played a large role in his climb through the ranks from an Army private.

He could also tell a tale or two, turning the ordinary into something colorful and memorable.

Golf was a common thread between us. My first recollections of him are from his days as a regular opponent of the late Perk Binney at the golf course in Brockway. Perk and his 3-iron dueled the Colonel and his Brownings over many a late-evening round of golf, some of which I was privileged to witness.

One of the more memorable golfing adventures the Colonel embarked on was with the late George Monaco as they shared a riding cart during a round of the Kersey Open.

On the trek from the 8th green at Brockway to the 9th

tee, as the cart rounded a bend, it tipped over, leaving the diminutive George to rescue the Colonel from underneath it. Both escaped injury.

In another Kersey Open moment, the Colonel scored a hole-in-one and, true to the conventions of the game, treated the field to a keg of liquid refreshment.

Time conspired to limit the Colonel's play over the last few years, but he relished every chance he did have to play. And though plagued by physical problems, he showed no bitterness. Trooper that he was, he played on, the next shot always the most important one.

Though neither of us realized it at the time, the Colonel was involved, indirectly, in my ultimate career path. After he retired from active duty, he took a supervisory position in the Indiana office of the state Department of Revenue. There was an opening for a field auditor and the Colonel encouraged me to apply.

Fresh out of college with a political science degree, I went about lining up the credentials I needed to compete for the job. There was another applicant, Sam Smith, whose father, L. Eugene "Snuffy" Smith, was the area's representative in the General Assembly. Sam got that job and, ultimately, succeeded his father in Harrisburg, where he is now an accomplished legislator. (He retired in 2015 after 28 years, the last four of them as Speaker of the House.)

I ended up in the newspaper business and, when not battling headlines or deadlines, got to spend time at the pro shop at Brockway GC with a lot of good people, including the Colonel.

During some trying times, the Colonel's quiet, sincere support did not go unnoticed.

When the seeds of the gulf war were sown in 1990, the Colonel told me he had provided infantry training in 1959 at

Fort Benning, Ga., to Jordan's King Hussein, who would play a crucial role in the conflict with Iraq. It was a good story, one of many the Colonel shared with me over the years.

The best story, however, is the life he lived and shared with a loving family and his legacy of duty and honor and devotion to them, to his God and his country.

The House Will Be In Order

Given the struggles that lay ahead of me, golf may have saved my life; there were a lot worse things that I could have been doing with all the time I spent on the course.

By 1985, I'd begun my career at the Courier-Express as a sportswriter. I was living life in the fast lane and the road ahead looked wide open. I was too busy to pay attention to the flashing lights that were warning me of a big detour up ahead.

Little did I know or imagine how much my interest – even obsession – with politics, civics and government would aid me in my newspaper career.

It wasn't supposed to work out quite like that.

I didn't know the whys and wherefores of the Vietnam War, but I knew it was on TV every night and that our soldiers were dying. I wrote a letter on a brown paper lunch bag and sent it President Johnson in the spring of 1968 … the year of the Tet Offensive and Johnson's decision not to seek re-election to the presidency.

I received a letter in reply on White House stationery from Whitney Shoemaker, Assistant to the President.

"President Johnson asked me to thank you for your letter. He wants you to know that he and his advisers are doing everything they can to bring peace to Viet-Nam. We

pray that our adversaries will soon agree with us that it would be better to settle our differences at the conference table – not on the battlefield."

My vow in Mrs. Moore's fifth-grade class to someday be President of the U.S. was still very much alive. I got involved in politics by the time I reached my teens. I attended school board and borough council meetings. I learned how local government works. I was secretary of the Brockway Democrat Club before I was old enough to vote.

In the spring of 1975, as the long sad saga of America's involvement in Vietnam came to an end, I walked through Brockway and polled 100 people, asking if they believed we should send more humanitarian aid and weapons to the South Vietnamese and commit more U.S. troops. The resounding answer was "No," which made news in the Courier-Express with a photo of me interviewing retired teacher Leona Bliss on her front porch.

I kept learning as much as I could, seeking out as many people as I could and making contacts and friends.

One of those friends was U.S. Congressman John P. Murtha. I wrote to him often about legislative matters and attended events when he came to town.

After my sophomore year at Penn State, I was looking for a summer internship. I wondered if there was something available in the nation's capital. So I asked.

He walked slowly and deliberately, his head down, his shoulders square, as he left the ornate trappings of the U.S. House chamber. As he neared the back of the room, he lifted his head and saw me waiting for him in the hallway.

"Your guests are here," I said, pointing to one of the small meeting rooms off the House floor where members could hold meetings when House business prevented them

from being in their offices. His furrowed brow relaxed. Jack Murtha looked at me. And he smiled.

Those were heady days in July 1981. The U.S. economy was rocked by recession. There was a new sheriff in Washington, a once-upon-a-time B movie actor named Ronald Reagan. Jack, a Democrat, had been re-elected to a fourth term in the House from the Johnstown-based 12th district, which at the time included Jefferson County and my hometown, Brockway.

I was about to enter my junior year at Penn State. Jack was entering the seventh of what turned out to be a 37-year stint in Congress, a tenure that ended with his death Monday at age 77.

While most of my contemporaries were busy with normal adolescent things in the 1970s, I swapped puppy love for politics, and that's how my path crossed Jack's. He and my socials studies teacher, John McNulty, were friends. Jack had been elected to the state House in 1968, the same year "Coach" McNulty lost narrowly in his bid to unseat Rep. L. Eugene Smith, the father of current Rep. Sam Smith.

By the time Jack became a congressman after Rep. John Saylor died in 1974, Coach and another history teacher, the late Clarence "Perk" Binney, had ignited my passion for politics and public service. Meeting and becoming friends with Murtha fanned the flames even more. I met him frequently, wrote to him constantly and dreamed of someday joining him on the Hill. As the summer of 1981 approached, I thought about the prospects of an internship in Washington. I had no idea what the procedure was so I took a shortcut and called Jack's home in Johnstown. He wasn't there but his wife, Joyce, said that someone would get back to me.

I ended up being awarded a Lyndon B. Johnson internship for July. The pay was $810, at a time when the

Nick Hoffman

vast majority of internships weren't paid. I was the only paid intern on Jack's staff that summer. I lived in a one-room flat at Georgetown University ($245 for the month), took the bus from Wisconsin Avenue to Capitol Hill each morning and went home the same route each evening.

Bean soup was my favorite lunchtime meal and I was a regular in the House cafeteria. I learned the tunnel system underneath the city's streets. Life goes on behind the scenes and, I learned quickly, underneath the scenes, too.

I worked on a number of projects that month with some of Jack's gifted staff, including his able LA (legislative aide), the late Bill Allen, as well as veterans affairs liaison Carm Scialaba. The education I didn't expect to get changed the course of my life more than any 30-day period except for my stay in alcohol rehab in Kansas in 1992.

The experience in 1981 showed me that I didn't have what it took to "succeed" as a congressional staffer. It can be and often is bitter, bruising and back-stabbing. The price was higher than I was willing to pay and I vowed when I came home to stay here if at all possible, a decision I've never regretted.

The congressman had trials of his own. Critics played "gotcha" and repeatedly assailed his tactics and dubbed him the "King of Pork." I say without reservation that Jack Murtha was not for sale. He didn't invent the monstrosity that passes for government today. He simply mastered it, because he worked more diligently and with more conviction than most of those around him.

If the culture in D.C. that is such a source of anger and frustration today is ever going to change, it has to start back here, at home, with us – and our expectations. Jack was a tireless advocate for this state and his district. His greatest virtue (among many) – loyalty – was seen by some *as a vulnerability, suggesting that he could be bought. He couldn't.*

An inscribed pewter cup that Jack gave me as a token of appreciation in 1981 sits on my bedroom dresser. Currently, it holds a boutonniere from my best friend's wedding and golf tees. But it will always be filled with admiration for a man who cast a bigger shadow in western Pennsylvania than even Punxsutawney Phil, one whose smile one summer afternoon off the House floor meant more to a young man from back home than he could ever know.

That internship changed my life in a very unexpected way. I received 6 independent study credits from Penn State. One of the requirements was to write a paper about the experience. It included these observations:

"In the long hours at night after work and on weekends, I had an opportunity to think about a number of aspects of life. I was lonely at times, and that loneliness made me acutely aware of the 'little things' that I have tended to take for granted.

"I've become so accustomed to the personal and amiable relationships that a small town offers that when those relationships failed to materialize in Washington, I felt alienated and frustrated.

"I never thought I had as much as I now realize that I do."

Better late than never.

I wasn't familiar then with the poems of Edgar Guest, but if I had been, I'm sure I'd have embraced "Hometown."

Some folks leave home for money
And some leave home for fame,
Some seek skies always sunny,
And some depart in shame.
I care not what the reason
Men travel east and west,

Or what the month or season —
The home-town is the best.

The home-town is the glad town
Where something real abides;
'Tis not the money-mad town
That all its spirit hides.
Though strangers scoff and flout it
And even jeer its name,
It has a charm about it
No other town can claim.

The home-town skies seem bluer
Than skies that stretch away,
The home-town friends seem truer
And kinder through the day;
And whether glum or cheery
Light-hearted or depressed,
Or struggle-fit or weary,
I like the home-town best.

Let him who will, go wander
To distant towns to live,
Of some things I am fonder
Than all they have to give.
The gold of distant places
Could not repay me quite
For those familiar faces
That keep the home-town bright.

Despite the rude awakening to the reality of life
outside the "peaceful, quiet valley" I grew up in, I did run
for political office. Once. For Brockway Borough Council
in 1983, fresh out of college. I didn't quite make it and

although I wasn't crestfallen, it was my first and last race. I quickly discovered that it was more fun to watch.

Working for the Courier-Express gave me that opportunity. Election nights were the best. Through the 1970s and '80s, we still used paper ballots. When the polls closed at 8 p.m., the local election workers painstakingly counted the votes and posted the totals on the door of the polling place. Then they packed up and went to the county seat, Brookville, where the votes were certified and the results announced.

Members of the media were allowed "inside the ropes," which usually meant nibbling on a meat and cheese tray in the commissioners' office, trying to get as much information as we could about what was going on behind the scenes.

There was no Internet yet, so people relied on newspaper and radio to give them the results. Being an afternoon publication gave us a few extra hours to get complete returns, and our coverage was as good as any and better than most.

Politics then was still mainly about people, knowing who your voters were and what they needed and how we could help them.

The Goldenrod Is Yellow

It is only 18 miles from Brockway to Brookville but it's hard to believe, politically, that they're even on the same planet. The beauty of growing up in rural America, though, is that they're all good people and politics is rarely a contact sport.

My hometown, Brockway, was a Democrat stronghold in overwhelmingly Republican Jefferson County. Brockway was made up of a large group of people with Eastern European and Italian roots, which also meant heavily Catholic. Both are pillars of the Democrat Party. As Brockway Glass grew, labor unions rose in prominence and influence. They, too, were a big Democrat constituency.

In the rest of Jefferson County, the main influences were Northern European, Protestant and agricultural – all very Republican. A good friend and I were discussing the state of politics in the county. He offered the very prescient observation that, in Brookville and the townships surrounding it, "Judas Iscariot could run and win, as long as he was a Republican."

Not until the early years of the 2000s did the county – formed in 1804 – elect a Democrat as its president judge.

Still, it was fascinating how socio-economic and

political forces expressed themselves, and I used my Aunt Helen to try to explain it a little more.

Like the Titanic, Aunt Helen has slipped away.

But unlike the ocean liner that sank in 1912 on its maiden voyage, Aunt Helen Repiscak was more indestructible and lasted longer. She was 4 ½ years old when the Titanic went down. She died last week at age 95 and all but the last month or so of the 1,142 months she spent on this earth were pretty good ones.

She never married. She never had a driver's license. She lived at the corner of Main and McCain streets in Brockway, a few hundred yards from St. Tobias Church, where she dutifully and faithfully practiced and proclaimed her religion. She worked for more than 40 years at Brockway Glass Plant 1.

She had the metabolism of a hummingbird, always flitting around from one chore to the next, cleaning and re-cleaning her home, sweeping and re-sweeping the steps and the sidewalk outside.

One of 10 children of John and Mary Repiscak, she was born, raised and lived and worked and prayed in Brockway until she moved to Christ the King Manor in DuBois in 1991.

Her parents came here from (what is now) Czechoslovakia around the turn of the 20ᵗʰ Century. Her mother lived to be 96, and Helen cared for her until her death in 1969.

Helen and her siblings were a hard working lot, as most of their contemporaries – immigrants or first generation children of immigrants – were.

For a political junkie like me, Aunt Helen was a living history lesson in the rise of the Democrat Party in America.

From the Civil War years of the 1860s until the Great Depression began in the late 1920s, America was almost uninterruptedly a Republican country. Political power flowed from material wealth, not from the people. U.S.

Senators weren't elected by popular vote until 1916. Labor unions and work rules were unheard of. You think money matters now? Take a look at its influence a hundred years ago. To this day, the GOP struggles to escape its lineage to that era.

As the 20th Century dawned, the sheer weight of the immigrant population and its progeny empowered the Democrats; the Depression years swept them into power on a tidal wave of popular support.

An energetic leader like Franklin D. Roosevelt was the icing on the cake and, until the last 10 years, the Democrats held a virtual stranglehold on the U.S. House of Representatives and the legislative process in this country.

Political sands shift, sometimes in obvious ways, more subtly at other times.

But as the late Speaker of the House Thomas P. "Tip" O'Neill said, "All politics is local."

For people like Aunt Helen, that was true.

The Democrats embraced her and millions like her. They, in turn, embraced the party.

On an intellectual level, it's arguable how much individual philosophy meshed with the party's.

But homes aren't built and families aren't fed on philosophy.

The Democrats, especially in Brockway where I grew up, ruled the roost. It was the most simple of compacts – you scratch my back and I'll scratch yours.

We're often advised that it's the "little things" that matter most, and the Democrats in Brockway understood that, and took full advantage of it. That's politics.

Aunt Helen could have walked a hundred or so yards from her home to the polling place. But she didn't have to.

The Democrats made sure she got a ride on Election Day. A specimen ballot was never far away in case someone wanted some insight on the choices they had to make. Usually, one "X" was sufficient.

We gave rides to the polls to those who needed or wanted them. We manned the phones and encouraged people to vote. We did all the things we knew how to do to add the personal touch. And we were rewarded, year after year.

To this day, in Republican Jefferson County, Brockway remains a Democrat stronghold. The gap has narrowed significantly over the last 20 years, but Democrats outnumber Republicans 751-510.

Party doesn't mean as much as it used to and parties don't – or can't – inspire the loyalty they once did.

The people of Aunt Helen's generation were grist for so many mills to some, but they were the lifeblood of the emerging Democrat Party. The bond between them has been passed on for generations and, though diluted, still exists today.

Even so, Aunt Helen was more to me than lubricant for a political machine.

She was the woman who, along with my Grandmother, logged enough miles "gallivanting" to circumnavigate the globe a few times. She was the woman who never left the house, even on the sunniest day, without unplugging the TV for fear a storm would blow up. She was the woman who taught me this little ditty about fall: "The goldenrod is yellow, the corn is turning brown; the trees in apple orchards with fruit are bending down."

She was a personality, a character in the truest sense and best sense; a "pistol" as one longtime friend of hers said.

From a distance, some may look at her life, despite its length, and conclude that she didn't do much of lasting value.

But as my Grandmother and I sobbed under a tent in the windswept chill at St. Tobias Cemetery Friday after one last ride together with Aunt Helen, we both knew better.

Indestructible? No.

Irreplaceable? Yes.

All Aboard For Buffalo

When I graduated from Penn State in 1983, I knew that my future would not involve a career on the PGA Tour and I abandoned the dream of being a politician.

So what was I going to do with my bachelor's degree, a minor in finance, a 3.41 GPA and University Scholar status?

The situation wasn't made any easier by the recession that had engulfed the nation. In the three-county area I called home, the **average** monthly unemployment rate for 1983 was 14.9%.

I was fortunate, however. Finishing up at Penn State required four trimesters of study at University Park in State College, about an hour from home. Most of my classes were Monday-Wednesday-Friday. Tuesdays and Thursdays were usually wide open.

I was less than enthusiastic about college. Despite the Nittany Lions football team winning its first national championship my senior year, I did not attend any games at Beaver Stadium. To this day, I have never been in the parking lot of the stadium. I root for Penn State (usually), but my life and happiness aren't tied to the fortunes of a football team or to things I can't exercise some control over. And the view of the games is better in the peace and quiet of my living room anyhow.

Rather than drive back and forth to the campus, I caught the Fullington Trailways bus in DuBois and let them do the driving to State College. A roundtrip ticket cost about $15. But I ended up paying a lot less.

The death last week of Jack Fritz of DuBois took me back more than 30 years to when he and I first met.

Among his many avocations, bowling was a particular favorite. He was a promoter, as was my Dad, who was the proprietor of Timber Lanes in Brockway until the early 1970s.

So it wasn't surprising that many of my early contacts were with people who knew my Dad. By the time I started commuting, via Fullington Trailways bus line, to University Park to finish my undergraduate work at Penn State, Jack's path and mine crossed.

Jack was looking for some weekend help at the counter of the bus terminal, which fronted Liberty Boulevard next to Mansell Stadium. He asked if I was interested. Of course I was, since the job included free rides to and from Penn State.

By the summer of 1982, I was working every day and learning as much about the industry as I wanted to. Among Jack's many talents was that of teacher.

I graduated in 1983 and, like many grads, faced that nagging question of "Now what?" Leave that to Jack. He needed a full-time assistant to help him, particularly in the area of revenue accounting. The business was growing; Fullington expanded from the Buffalo-Pittsburgh line to Cleveland and Williamsport and Harrisburg. A lot of people depended on intercity service in those days and we were charged with providing it.

Jack knew the business. He knew to the penny how much revenue it took per mile to break even. There was much more to it, including tweaking schedules and managing

He Was There All the Time

drivers and mechanics and working hand-in-hand with the late John Lacny, Fullington's vice president.

Jack taught; I learned. He and his wife May made it fun. There were tough days, especially in winter or any day that buses were running late or breaking down. There is a world of difference between driving a bus and being a bus driver and that was never more evident than during the Greyhound strike in 1983. That put a lot more stress on small carriers like Fullington but Jack and John and the pros who drove them did heroic things to keep the buses running.

I went to work for Jack for $200 a week, my first full-time job. I should say I went to work "with" Jack. He had a quality of never making me feel like he was my boss, even though he was. We worked together, and that made all the difference.

My only trip to New York City was with Jack for a Trailways conference. The cab ride through the caverns of Midtown Manhattan left a lasting impression ... I haven't been back since.

While Jack hoped I'd make a career out of it, he was nothing but supportive when the Courier-Express came calling in early 1984, wondering if I'd be interested in a sportswriting position. I was, and that gig lasted 30 years, until last summer.

Over the years, Jack and I saw less of each other, usually when it had something to do with bowling. The memories never wore out, though. May and I remembered Tuesday at the Goble-Baronick Funeral Home and, as we almost always managed to do, worked in a chuckle or two.

One of the things I learned quickly was how to give a "lane call," such as the evening departure to Buffalo, N.Y. "Buffalo coach now loading in Lane 3; Sabula, Penfield, Byrnedale, St. Marys, Johnsonburg, Kane, Bradford,

Salamanca, Ellicotville, Springville and Buffalo. Buffalo coach now loading in Lane 3!"

Jack taught; I learned. Once more, for old time's sake, "Fritz coach now loading; Osceola Mills, Korea, Texarkana, A&P, Trailways, Jo May, DuBois Lanes, NASCAR, May, John and Lori, Jeff and Jill, John 'JD,' Cory, Abby, Adam and Tyler Fritz; Jaxon and Jordan. All aboard!"

Meet The Press

I enjoyed my time at the bus terminal, and was prepared to stay longer. But one afternoon, the assistant sports editor at the Courier-Express, Bantley Myers, stopped by and told me they were looking for a full-time sportswriter. Before they advertised the job, the publisher and editors decided to ask me if I would be interested. If I was and we could make a deal, the job was mine.

As long as I can remember, I was in love with newspapers. Dad and Mom and my brother Kevin, sister Penny and me occupied the second and third floors of our home; Nan and Papa had the downstairs.

Our kitchen/dining room was on the second floor. Dad recalled coming home to find me on the kitchen floor with the newspaper spread in front of me, imploring him to read it to me.

Eventually, he was propping me on his lap and letting me read the Courier-Express to him. I remember one edition that told of a mine explosion in West Virginia around Thanksgiving.

Years later, I Googled it and found that it was the Farmington mine disaster in which 78 miners perished. It happened a week before Thanksgiving in 1968.

I couldn't wait for the paper. Pearl and Wendell Moody operated a variety store on Main Street in Brockway.

Nick Hoffman

Not only could you find the DuBois, Bradford and Punxsutawney papers, but the two Pittsburgh papers – the Post-Gazette and Press – were there, too, along with The Grit, a weekly magazine that was quite popular. Cable TV was in its infancy, radio still a presence, the Internet hadn't arrived. Newspapers were very important in the fabric of life.

I'd hang out on Main Street, especially on Saturdays in the winter, waiting for the delivery of that day's bundles, which included the Press, which I'd take home and devour as ravenously as I would a turkey dinner.

Moody's and the town's two pharmacies – Brockway Drug and Gillung's Pharmacy – had the best candy counters any kid could want. All three were on the same block, just across Main Street from each other. Maybe that is why one of the three dentists in town had his office in the middle of them.

It wasn't surprising that I moved on from The Buzzer, our high school paper, to the weekly Brockway Record and finally The Courier. In fact, I intended to study journalism at Penn State, but decided I wanted to be an attorney and changed to political science.

I'd written on and off for the Courier in high school and college. They knew my work, and since the spring sports season was about to begin, they didn't want to go into it short-handed.

I asked for $250 a week. They offered $235. Good enough. I was following in Dad's footsteps. He'd also written for the Brockway Record and the Courier around the time he and mom were married in 1959. I had a lot of supporters at the newspaper – general managers Bill Reay and Marv Bloom among them. They knew Dad, as did Herb Martin.

Herb Martin, this newspaper's guiding editor for four decades, died Thursday.

Herb's titles were "editor" in various incarnations: sports, news, managing, even "senior."

But Herb's true genius was as a teacher, in his own writing and in what he taught those of us who carry on his work.

In newsrooms of small daily newspapers, the demands of deadline and production add a unique degree of intimacy to co-worker relationships.

In short, no one can do it alone; editors, reporters and photographers go beyond working together and learn to rely on one another.

That's one of the lessons Herb taught me in the nearly 30 years that we collaborated at this newspaper. Even after his retirement, we compared notes on issues and events. I valued his counsel and enjoyed his company.

He was remarkable in many ways.

His index fingers-only method of typing wasn't "by the book" but it was as fast and accurate as any method I ever saw.

He was a pack rat. It took as many dump trucks to clean his office out when we moved to our new headquarters as it did to clean the rest of 54 W. Long Ave.

He was a good-hearted, mild-mannered, fun-loving man, qualities that gave him a rare air of humanity in the rough-and-tumble newspaper business.

Herb was also possessed of a hearty guffaw. The rest of us laughed, but Herb was always guffawing.

As sports editor, managing editor and senior editor, Herb surely fielded his share of angry or indignant callers. Those are tough; exasperating when it is our fault and aggravating when it isn't.

Of all the qualities Herb possessed, his patience and

Nick Hoffman

his ability to deflect or defuse otherwise volatile situations were the most admirable.

I don't remember ever seeing him lose his cool. Ever.

One thing Herb did have trouble keeping were verbs. It was one of his idiosyncrasies that so many of his headlines were verb-less. Instead of saying, "He was a great guffawer," Herb would write it, "A great guffawer he."

When we received the news of Herb's death Thursday morning, someone asked me what we should do to pay homage.

"Put out a front page without any verbs in the headlines," I said, half chuckling, half choked up.

Herb played a big role in my entry into this profession.

He and my Dad worked together in the 1950s when Herb and Dean Close were broadcasting football games on WKBI, St. Marys.

When Herb came to DuBois as our sports editor, he and Dad shared some great sports moments together, and stories filled the Courier-Express sports pages for days.

When the newspaper needed a part-time sportswriter to help with Brockway coverage, I graduated from the Brockway Record to the C-E in the mid-1970s under the auspices of the late John Klees, then sports editor.

I sniffed out a few news stories, too, including one on police salaries that went to court over a public records issue and got Herb and me in a little hot water over the content of the story. I was wrong. Herb helped me to fix it and I learned.

When I joined the staff full-time in 1984, the sports desk I shared with Sports Editor Bantley Myers was right next to Herb's cubbyhole.

When the opportunity came to go to the "news side" in 1987 as news manager at our Brockville Bureau, Herb supported me.

He Was There All the Time

We had a lot of fun in the ensuing years, chronicling the complex, the bizarre, the zany and everything in between.

This business isn't always easy or rewarding, but pros like Herb had a way of making you want to come back for more, even after a bad day. Being a newspaperman was more than a job; it was an obligation and a privilege.

The microfilm records will preserve his tenure at our newspaper for all time to come.

Our hearts will hold fond memories of Herb for a lot longer.

Getting To Know You

Anyone who seriously contemplates a career in media, especially newspapers, has to be curious and personable. The most accomplished writer, the biggest vocabulary and most jocular personality are worthless if not accompanied by curiosity, the trait I consider the most indispensable for a journalist.

Jason Gray Sr., the father of the publisher who hired me, often asked Bill Reay, his advertising manager "what the boys downtown were saying."

He knew, as Bill did, that a good newspaper has to be in touch with the people it serves and what matters to them. That isn't easy, but it's essential.

Too often as we get older, we lose touch with the people around us, especially the younger ones. I've read histories from ancient Rome in which a philosopher of one generation would foretell doom once the "young people" took the reins of leadership.

It never hurts to pause and take a look around and make sure we haven't allowed our universe to become too small.

I've logged a lot of miles this spring and summer by starting a routine of walking 2 ½ to 3 ½ miles as often as I can, preferably daily.

I can walk from my house to the post office in Brockway

and back, or park my car at Martino's Bi-Lo and make three round trips to the post office and get my 3 ½ miles in.

If I don't stop to talk to Peter Varischetti or Jim Manners or Moose and Punkie Verne or Dave Benson or Teet Mancini or the "boys" on the Sportsmen's Club porch or any one of countless others whose paths I cross, I can do 3 ½ miles in one hour.

But, as often as not, I have to stop and talk – that's half the fun.

I've started making it a point to say "hi" to the young people along Main Street, whether they're in Martino's parking lot or along the sidewalk in front of Fox's Pizza or Paesano's or in front of the former site of Jack's Men's Wear.

Not that many years ago, it was Paesano's or the Rover Room for me. In my Dad's day, it was the City Restaurant, among other venues.

Now, some people express dismay at young people "loafing" along Main Street, seeing what kind of trouble they can get into, surmising that those kids probably won't amount to too much.

Well, here's a flash for you. Being a teen-ager is enough trouble without looking for any more.

I remember how scared I was. Couldn't dance. Acne. Never enough money. No car. Algebra. And, of course, the other little things like 'What am I going to do with my life?" or the flip side, "What's life going to do to me?" Job? Marriage? Kids? Etc., etc.

I mean, how much worse can it get?

Maybe I am naïve, but I don't worry much about this "crisis" among today's youth, about the challenges they face and their lack of preparedness or ability to rise to the occasion.

Somebody probably said that about my grandparents' generation. All they did was rebuild the nation from the

Nick Hoffman

depths of the Great Depression, take a breath, then fight and win World War II.

A generation or so later, many were saying all was lost when the "hippies" took to the streets to protest our involvement in the Vietnam war before turning their ire on Richard Nixon and his thugs. Turned out they knew better than most.

Granted, my generation hasn't faced war, pestilence or economic calamity. Quite the contrary, we've been busy trying to figure out to how preserve (or waste) the peace and prosperity made possible by our predecessors.

So what about today's kids?

They'll be just fine, especially if, for the time being, we leave them alone and let them be kids. They'll figure most of it out by themselves just like you did. Just like I did.

A few will fall off the radar screen and end up in jail or in a gutter somewhere. But the natural order of things dictates that someone has to fill those slots. Not rooting against anybody, of course, but that's life – some of us don't choose as well as others.

Others will die untimely deaths – my class has buried too many already and we haven't celebrated our 25th reunion yet.

But most will get over their skin conditions, buy pants that don't have holes in them, get better car stereo systems and "grow up" and marry and raise families and get jobs (and pay lots of Social Security taxes to ensure my comfort in old age.)

We need to get to know them.

One of them may someday be tuning up my car engine, another could be doing my taxes while another might be cleaning my teeth or filling cavities (Yikes! Remember "Marathon Man"?)

It was reassuring to me when I was a kid listening to older folks talk about growing up.

The details were different but, "They went through some of what I'm going through. Must be possible to survive this."

So on my walks through town, I make it a point to say hello to these kids, to let them know that, by and large, "been there, done that."

They're different in some ways, but in ways that matter more, they're very much the same.

And there's some reassurance in that.

Teach Me To Number My Days, Too

When you grow up in a small town in rural America, it's easy to be irritated that everyone knows your business, as opposed to an urban area where few people if any know – or care – if you're alive as long as you don't cut them off in rush hour traffic.

There is a bright side, though. It is comforting that when times get tough – illness, loss of a job, death – that people in a small town know and care what you're going through.

God promises in Revelation 21:7 that "He who overcomes shall inherit all things, and I will be his God and he shall be My son."

Easier said than done, if we forget that the premise of the promise is that we embrace the gift of salvation through the death and resurrection of Jesus Christ.

Anyone who claims that God is his or her co-pilot is sitting in the wrong seat.

We look at others to see how they deal with situations, to see if we can learn a thing or two. I believe that what "defines" us shouldn't be what we achieve, but rather what we overcome, which is a restatement of the "life is a journey not a destination" theory.

Good things, they say, come in small packages. George Monaco was a diminutive man who did a lot of good things for a lot of people.

My first encounter with George came, I think, in early 1973. That spring, I had decided I wanted to play baseball. God only knows why. I'd never played baseball in my life. I was a chubby 11-year-old who had about as much athletic ability as a doorknob. Problem was, I didn't know that.

George did.

I remember George telling me after the first couple nights of tryouts that I wasn't going to survive the "cut." He encouraged me to practice and work hard. Looking back, he probably should have gotten a Nobel Prize for diplomacy.

My next encounter with George came on another athletic field, this time, the golf course. That was a venue that was very special to both George and me. We shared a lot of good times with a lot of good people.

George was one of the men who was responsible for what is now Owens-Brockway Golf Course being constructed. He and I sat around the pro shop many nights telling stories about the "early days," because my grandfather helped out some in those days, too.

For several years, George was secretary-treasurer of the men's Tuesday night golf league. That will test anyone's tact and diplomacy. It probably tested George's, too, but he never showed it. He found the "happy medium" in life and lived within it.

Despite his small stature, George was a very accomplished golfer. He had a distinct pre-shot routine, which all golfers are encouraged to have, but few do.

He hit the ball straight, kept it in play and made a lot of good pars with some creative chipping and putting. You learned quickly that George didn't need too many strokes *in the inveterate golfers' side-bets games - and didn't want them, either.*

No matter what it was - baseball, golf, sounding Taps on Memorial Day or Veterans Day at an American Legion program, playing in the band - George gave it everything he had.

I remember being his partner a number of years ago in an early season best-ball event. George knocked his tee shot on Number 1 out of bounds. He repeated his pre-shot routine and put the next one in play. He was lying 3 at that point on a par 4 hole. He then stroked his approach onto the green and drained the putt for a bogey 5. Many golfers go bananas when they hit it OB, especially on the first hole. Ruins the day, you know. But not for George.

Maybe that's because George knew how to number his days. Some years ago, he fought a successful battle against the cancer that claimed him this week. That was George; battling back, refusing to quit and keeping his sense of humor, too.

His wife, Lucy, told me Sunday at the funeral home that he tried so hard these last few weeks to keep fighting.

It wasn't that George didn't have any fight left. There just weren't any more rounds left to fight.

There were a lot of people at the funeral home Sunday night to pay their respects to George. That's as it should have been. He brightened a lot of lives and left a lot of memories.

The Lady Would Not Yield

There are people who bear a burden that lasts a lifetime and persevere despite unrelenting pain and sorrow. Their stories inspire us.

I don't have a clear memory of the rape and murder of a young high school student by one of her teachers in DuBois in 1966. I eventually learned about it ... and of the courage and dignity of the victim's mother.

Our "runover" page on Sundays is typically full of obituaries, due to the larger area (seven counties) we circulate in versus weekdays and the absence of a Saturday edition.

Last week, there was only one obituary. "LaVonne Marie Rimer of Luthersburg died Thursday at DuBois Regional Medical Center following a short illness," it read.

A couple paragraphs later, the obituary continued, "She was also preceded in death by . . . a daughter, Pamela Sue Rimer . . ."

I worked Saturday night and placed that obituary on Page A 11. I paused, and reflected.

My phone rang Monday morning. The caller asked if I was familiar with Mrs. Rimer's situation. I knew, I told him, but Mrs. Rimer's obituary didn't need mention of the anguish she never sought but bravely endured for 44 years.

Nick Hoffman

In late April 1966, Pamela Sue Rimer was murdered by her math teacher at DuBois Area High School, Jon E. Yount.

That case is the first high-profile murder in this area that I have any memory of from my childhood. Since then, I've seen and covered more murders and murder trials than I can recount and one thing that they all have in common is how the murderers' names seem to outlive and outlast their victims. Billings. Edmiston. Renchenski. Spotz, to name a few.

This case was different. Mention "Jon Yount" and many people will respond "Pam Rimer."

The Daily Collegian at Penn State wrote about the story in 1994 in which Mrs. Rimer said Yount stole her life and her family's. Her son was killed in a farming accident three years before Pamela Sue was murdered.

Afterward, her husband went insane and died. She said she now has nothing; no children or grandchildren. No one calls to see how she's doing. Her life, she said, is effectively over and the only thing that keeps her alive is caring for her mother.

People who knew of Yount said he was a cruel man, according to The Daily Collegian. Mrs. Rimer asked her daughter why she was trying to get out of his class; Pamela Sue told her, "You ought to see his eyes."

Senior Retired Clearfield County Judge John K. Reilly Jr. was the district attorney who prosecuted Yount in two trials, both of them ending in convictions for first-degree murder.

Reilly said this week that he remembers LaVonne Rimer as a "very lovely lady who had more than her share of tragedy" but handled it, despite her suffering, "gracefully." She earned his admiration, Reilly said, and the fact that Yount, now 72, is still locked up is "amazing," due in no small measure to LaVonne Rimer's devotion to seeing justice for her daughter.

Yount admitted the crime but adamantly disputed the degree of murder. The Daily Collegian interviewed him, too. Yount said he thought he'd paid his debt after serving 20 years. That's when he walked away from the state prison at Rockview with his girlfriend, Diane Brodbeck.

The pair was captured 2 ½ years later in Idaho and odds are Yount will spend the rest of his life in prison.

Judge Reilly said he doesn't know what the average length of a "life" sentence is in Pennsylvania, but the fact that Yount is still behind bars is "amazing."

The fact that he is still in prison is due in large part to the devoted efforts of LaVonne Rimer, who spearheaded opposition to efforts to secure clemency or a pardon for Yount.

Only God knows what LaVonne Rimer, a Catholic by faith according to her obituary, felt in the depths of her soul.

My instinct tells me it was less about vengeance than it was justice for her daughter.

Jon Yount may never grasp that; LaVonne Rimer never forgot it.

My hope and prayer is that she finds the peace that eluded her for so long in life.

Mrs. Rimer died in 2010. Jon Yount died in prison two years later; he hanged himself in his cell two days before the anniversary of Pamela Sue Rimer's death.

Mrs. Rimer did not yield.

The Solider And The Sugar Cookie

It doesn't always take a tragedy like the one Mrs. Rimer endured to leave an impression. I know of an instance where a sugar cookie in the midst of a world war was enough.

I kept my hand inside my coat, clutching the package as I walked toward her. She was seated in a chair near the casket bearing her husband at the Goble-Baronick Funeral Home in DuBois Monday afternoon.

Irene Sheldon looked up and said, "You have sugar cookies, don't you?"

I nodded and revealed a package of Archways.

We chuckled. We hugged. We cried.

"Put them in with him," Irene said. "He'd like that."

• • •

William "Red" Sheldon died Saturday at age 84.

After he retired from Bell Telephone, Red, an avid golfer, went to work part-time in the pro shop at Owens Brockway Golf Course for my partner, Jim Beimel Sr., and me in the late 1980s and early 1990s.

I didn't know about the sugar cookies then.

What I did know was how much Red and Irene enjoyed late summer afternoons on the golf course, often in the company of the late Bob McIntosh and his wife Vada, or maybe the late Bill Nosker and his wife Ethel, or John Verne and his late wife Helen or Bob and Dot Martino or some of the many others whose presence made a lot of long Sundays more pleasant for me.

It wasn't until years later I found out about the sugar cookies.

Red was a U.S. Army veteran of World War II. He served 18 months in Europe and received numerous citations, including the Victory Medal, the Rifle Sharpshooter Award, the European, African, Middle East Campaign with three battle stars and the Good Conduct Medal.

Actually, Red earned the medals during the war but he didn't receive them until 58 years later, in 2003. A technicality prevented them from being awarded right after the war. Through the efforts of his son Bill, one thing led to another and Red finally got his medals.

Chris Taylor wrote a story in the Dec. 21, 2003, edition of Tri-County Sunday about Red's medals. It included this vignette.

"Although he was only miles away from the Battle of the Bulge, it wasn't the falling 'buzz bombs' that made a lasting impression on him.

"It was the resiliency and kindness of the German people ... Later in the winter, Sheldon made direct contact with a German family.

"We were billeted with civilians. My squad had 13 fellas and we stayed with a pharmacist," he said.

"It was the night before Christmas, and these people invited us into their kitchen and gave the boy a key.

"He went in and unlocked a door to the living room

where you got into on a special occasion. He came back with a tin box, and we all got a sugar cookie.

"To this day, Sheldon's favorite dessert remains sugar cookies."

That Christmas, and several since, a package showed up at Red and Irene's home on West Garfield Avenue.

I didn't make it to their home last Christmas and I didn't get to deliver the cookies until Monday. Red would understand.

How's this for a Top 10 list? Red Sheldon: Golfer (that says a lot about anyone), Free Mason, 36-year employee of Bell Telephone, Lakeside Methodist Church member, World War II veteran, friend, grandfather, father, husband, son.

In 84 years, he embraced the best and endured the worst that life has to offer, always with a smile.

For Red, like so many members of his generation, life was a straightforward equation that applied in any situation: Faith, family, duty, country, integrity.

I can't offer a snappy salute to Red as a comrade in arms because the service and sacrifice by him and our Armed Forces allowed me to grow up and live in a world of relative peace, one in which I am free to write stories, express opinions, vote, worship and otherwise bask in the fruits of freedom.

I have no musical talent, so I can't coax "Taps" from a bugle or caress "Amazing Grace" from a set of bagpipes.

I don't have much of a sweet tooth anymore either. But, when the spirit moves me, I enjoy a good sugar cookie as much as anyone.

Except Red.

Bon Appetit!

If not a sugar cookie, a ham and cheese sandwich can taste mighty good sometimes.

I thought about the memories and meals Ralph Yanity made for me while I was addressing a Christmas card to him last week.

Sadly, Ralph died at age 90 before he could celebrate Christmas this year.

To say that Ralph left a good taste in your mouth would be more than adequate for the man who fed thousands of students during his tenure as cafeteria manager for the Brockway Area School District.

When I started school in 1967, $1.75 a week bought five hot lunches. By the time I graduated, I think the tab was $2.40 or so.

Hot, nutritious and homemade to boot. Ralph was a soft-spoken, gentle, compassionate man who, along with a dedicated staff, took the job of feeding the students seriously.

Even after I graduated high school, for the two years I lived at home and attended Penn State DuBois, it wasn't unheard of for me to stop by the high school and eat with some of the teachers in the faculty dining room, especially if the menu featured Ralph's scrumptious turkey, gravy and mashed potatoes. Yummmmm!

I don't remember any "bad" lunches. Everyone had

their favorites, and toasted cheese sandwiches took a lot of good-natured kidding when they were referred to as "bricks."

I, for one, never left the cafeteria hungry.

Things have changed in the lunch lines of the 21st century, and not for the better.

Golf was played in the spring back then, in the days before buses or vans took teams to matches. Two or three players who had cars loaded the rest of us up with them to go to Punxsutawney or St. Marys or Brookville. That would never fly today.

Before we left on those road trips, Ralph would make sure we had a supply of meat and cheese sandwiches, figuring that we'd be getting home late and might not have time to grab a bite.

Ralph and his staff weren't teachers, but his kitchen and cafeteria were just as integral to the schools as were classrooms, chalkboards and faculty.

Someone recalled Ralph saying that lunch might be the only hot meal some of those kids got a day and he wanted to make sure they got a good one.

I thought about that in light of the furor over what to do with refugees fleeing the carnage in Syria. Should we take some in or deny them all?

I find myself torn about what to do. There are risks in doing something, and in doing nothing.

But I think I know what Ralph Yanity would do. He'd set a few extra places, prepare a little extra food and make sure they got a good, hot meal. It might be the only one they got, and it might be the only time they felt like someone cared. For him, I believe, that would be a risk worth taking.

He wasn't a teacher in the conventional sense. But his approach to his life's work was an object lesson for us to digest.

Bon appétit, Mr. Yanity

Long Live The Queen!

A lady from "The Valley" – between DuBois in Clearfield County and Byrnedale in Elk County – was affectionately known to many as "The Queen."

She and her husband were stewards of the Civilian Conservation Corps (CCC) museum at Parker Dam State Park. There aren't many of them left, but what they did will bear witness to who they were long after the last one is gone.

Friday was "her day," her 90th birthday.

And like so many days in her long life, Helen Adams of Penfield spent part of it reaching out to her many friends, sharing her happiness and enthusiasm with them.

Dressed in blue slacks, a red T-shirt, white purse and a red, white and blue umbrella, Helen made the rounds at her favorite store, Shop and Save at The Commons, meeting and greeting everyone with her trademark smile and infectious enthusiasm.

"Keep smiling. Tomorrow's another day," she said as she made her rounds, much like a doctor making her rounds with a vaccination needle.

"I know things are tough for a lot of people," she said, adding that a smile or a hug can cure a lot of ills.

She would know.

She and her late husband Lou were the King and Queen

of the CCC Boys, organizing and staging an annual reunion for those who worked at the camp in Penfield during the Great Depression.

The camps and the "boys" are legend, borne of the cruel joblessness and poverty that swept the nation in the early 1930s.

The Civilian Conservation Corps was one of the linchpins of President Franklin D. Roosevelt's New Deal.

Millions of people found work and provided for their families in the public works project. Roads, bridges, state parks and more were built in a massive program that stabilized the economy and restored hope to a despairing people.

The state Department of Conservation and Natural Resources described the effort on its website:

"Many young men came to the camps hungry and poorly clothed. They were issued uniforms and given three meals a day. Most young men gained about 40 pounds while in the CCC. The men earned $30 a month, most of which was sent home to their families.

"Run by the U.S. Army, the regimented life of camp was new to most new enrollees. A typical day began at 6 a.m. with breakfast at 6:30 a.m. followed by sick call and policing of the camp. At 7:15 a.m. trucks were loaded with tools and men for the day. "Local experienced men" usually served as foremen for the work. Lunch was usually half of an hour. At 4 p.m. the trucks headed back to camp for the flag lowering ceremony, inspection and announcements. After dinner, the men had free time until lights out at 10 p.m.

"The U.S. Army ran the camps, but foresters, carpenters and other people directed the work. The CCC fought forest fires, planted trees, built roads, buildings, picnic areas, swimming areas, campgrounds and

created many state parks. When not working, the men socialized and had opportunities to learn crafts and skills."

There were 113 camps in Pennsylvania, including Ridgway, Kane, Sheffield, Marienville, Cook Forest, Brockway, Caledonia, Clearfield, Penfield, Medix Run, Dent's Run, Sizerville, Wycoff Run, Punxsutawney and Sligo.

Lou and Helen were instrumental in the development of the CCC museum at Parker Dam State Park.

Lou died a few years ago, but Helen has carried on the mission of "reaching out" and "lifting up" anyone and everyone around her, helped by the constant and devoted attention of her caretaker, Bill Crawford.

Her advice Friday was, "keep moving; turn the TV off and get out and do something."

To know Helen is not to know royalty in the literal sense. Rather, it is to know nobility of spirit and soul, a hopeful determination and self-sufficiency that would go a long way to curing the nation's ills now, just as it did more than 75 years ago.

Long live the Queen.

True Grit

C ould the current crop of Americans duplicate the courage and grit of the Greatest Generation if called upon to do so?

I'd like to think we could, but I have to say I doubt it.

"Grit" isn't a word we hear too often anymore. When I think of grit, Al Tamin comes to mind.

Thursday was a long, sad day in the wake of the news that Alfred Tamin of Brockway had died.

Al and his wife, Lucette, retired proprietors of the BP Inn restaurant and bar in Brockport, are dear friends, as are their children, Carl and Caroline "Kiki" Tamin.

Honest, hardworking and fun-loving were Al's standout traits. Those weren't easy to cultivate in a business where he often saw some of his customers in some of their worst condition or behavior.

Al worked the bar, Lucette the kitchen. They'd often as not open up in the morning after coming in early to clean, and Al would often be there to close up.

I spent a lot of time in the BP, sometimes too much time. On those occasions, Al made sure I got home safely.

He saw a lot but said very little, preferring to keep his opinions to himself unless asked.

But there were exceptions.

One Sunday afternoon in mid-December, as a bunch of

us watched an NFL playoff game, the building shook with a loud thud and left us wondering "What was that?"

A patron who was a little too full of high-test had driven his truck a little too close to, or rather into, the side of the building. He and his passenger came in, bellied up to the bar and ordered drinks.

In his unmistakable style, punctuated with a heavy northern Italian accent, Al read them their pedigree.

When the kitchen end of the business expanded into pizzas, a couple young thugs figured they could put one over on old Al.

They'd call and order a pizza, pick it up, go home and devour it, then call back later complaining that the last pizza they'd ordered had a burnt crust. It worked. Once. The second time, they got an earful.

Al was tough when he had to be, but always fair.

He was pretty good football picker, too.

Several of us used to pick NFL games and Al had a knack for being in the thick of things at the top of the standings.

I was having a particularly difficult year and was in real jeopardy of having to wash dishes at our season-ending grand finale, a chore reserved for the two worst pickers.

For 15 weeks, I picked the Dallas Cowboys against whomever they played. For 15 straight weeks, they lost.

As the 16th and final week approached, Al told me to use my head and pick the Redskins, reasoning that I needed every win I could get, which I did.

I acceded to Al's pleas and picked the Redskins. Dallas won. Nobody's perfect.

A few years ago, too much time in too many bars left me with some tough decisions to make. Al was among those who stood by me and encouraged me.

He came to this country from Italy, carved out a life for

himself and his family, made friends, earned respect and managed to laugh more than he cried.

The good-bye came too quickly.

What will last much longer is my admiration for a man who not only "talked the talk," as all good bartenders do, but who "walked the walk," too.

It was a privilege to do both with him.

Who Spends Himself In A Worthy Cause

There was a time when I thought I had to "make it big" to matter, that it is all about fame and fortune if we want to validate our existence.

My great-grandfather was born in 1893 and died in 1980 at age 87. Bubba came to America on a wooden boat, mined 36-inch coal, worked at a clay factory, saw two World Wars and a Great Depression and lived to see man on the moon.

If I am blessed to live 87 years, what differences will I see? I've already witnessed the birth of cable TV, the Internet and cellphones, which don't sound like big deals to younger generations, but to those of us who grew up with aerials and rotary phones, it's mind-bending.

We're living longer, too. By most measures we're better educated and more affluent than our parents.

What's propping it all up is what concerns me. The pillars of the times Bubba and my grandparents and my Dad knew remained intact for the most part: Faith. Family. Education. Government.

Today, more people are moving away from, rather than toward, Christianity. The family is anything but a "unit." Education is in trouble. Our government is corrupt and gridlocked. Debt is everywhere, and growing.

When Dad lectured me in my adolescence about succumbing to peer pressure, he'd conclude his case by asking, "If everybody else jumped off the Golden Gate Bridge, would you?"

"Of course not, Dad," I'd say, not sure if I was trying to convince him ... or me.

"Making it big" rarely happens by design. In my experience, hard work, honesty and determination are the foundations on which rich lives are built. The best example I know of in that regard is Frank Varischetti.

***It is not the critic who counts,
not the man who points out
how the strong man stumbled,
or where the doer of deeds could have done better.***

So many times in so many places, the headline-grabbers are those who are as likely to be part of a problem as part of a solution.

In Brockway, in Frank Varischetti Sr., who died Thursday, that was not the case.

Those who knew of him might cite his success as his defining quality.

Those who knew him would point instead to the richness of his life and the value of his friendship.

A "doer of deeds;" that was Frank.

Problem? Solution. Do it!

Red tape was something to wrap Christmas packages with, not something to wade through.

Dr. Jim Devlin, Brockway Area High School's team physician and the 2002 Sportsman of the Year, spent a lot of time with Frank, especially on the sidelines at Rover football games. He paid tribute to Frank earlier this year and said of his friend's philosophy, "Dream big. Work hard. Have fun."

Frank didn't know what "can't" meant. He probably didn't even know it was a word – or an option.

But he did know how to work and how to play and he did them both with relish. It was a simple and effective approach to life that he and his wife Barbara passed on to their sons: Frank Jr., Steve, Peter and Nick. The Varischetti legacy is in good hands.

The credit belongs to the man who is actually in the arena; whose face is marred by dust and sweat and blood; who strives valiantly; who errs and comes short again and again.

Frank didn't start at the top.

When he was named Brockway's Citizen of the Year a couple years ago, correspondent Jim Grant described Frank's early years.

After graduating from Ridgway High School in 1957, he went to work on the construction of Route 153 over the mountain from Brockport to Penfield and spent his nights running a road roller. His dad gave him a tractor, which he traded in for an old Ford backhoe. He added a Studebaker dump truck to his stock and went into business for himself, digging ditches and hauling dirt.

He bought George Morrison's garbage truck and list of customers; Varischetti Sanitation was born. The business grew and Frank eventually accepted an offer from Browning-Ferris Industries in 1986 to buy the business, which by then included Greentree Landfill in Fox Township, Elk County, between Brockway and Kersey.

Who knows the great enthusiasms,
the great devotions and
spends himself in a worth course;

Frank remembered his roots and never forgot what it was to need. Money only enabled him to do more for those around him, to offer a helping hand or a word of encouragement.

His generosity knew no bounds. Church, community, school, friends, even strangers – all benefited from his presence in their midst. He gave what he had and gave of himself out of an obligation to a higher calling.

It wasn't all work and no play for Frank, though. He loved golf.

At last year's Dr. Quinn Lundberg Memorial Golf Tournament, Doug Grieneisen, Randy Taylor, Jeff Bille and I faced Frank, Nick Varishcetti, Eddy Inzana and Mark Becker in a playoff for the championship.

On the 1st hole, Randy drove the green of the par 4 hole and we scored a two-putt birdie. Nick, Eddy and Mark didn't quite reach the green. Frank got to tee off from the gold, or senior, tees.

I rode ahead and unintentionally cut in front of Frank, who yelled, "Fore!" to shoo me out of the way.

Embarrassed, I wandered over to him as he stood in the fairway preparing to hit his pitch shot. I "demanded" to see proof that he was old enough to use the gold markers.

"I'm 62 and half dead," he deadpanned, flashing his trademark grin at me.

He was never younger or more alive than that afternoon.

He put his team's second shot on the green and, for an encore, made the birdie putt to extend the playoff. He thrived on competition.

At the 2nd, Frank and I set up our team's respective birdie tries.

Putting third, Doug rolled in a 20-footer for our 3.

Nick Varischetti, batting last, rolled in a do-or-die 7-footer to halve the hole. Like father, like son.

At the 3rd, Eddy took advantage of Mark's second shot and set the team up with a 12-footer for birdie.

Doug, batting cleanup for us, hit his pitch to within 6 feet.

Frank's team just missed birdie before Doug rolled in the winning putt for us.

**And who, at worst, if he fails,
at least fails while daring greatly.**

Standing a few yards back from the green, Frank said matter-of-factly, "That's it," when he saw Doug's putt get close.

It wasn't surrender, just recognition that their best wasn't good enough today ... but there was always tomorrow.

Even then, Frank was fighting for his life, but whether it was the disease or a long, hard par 4, he poured everything he had into both.

Step up to the plate. Take your swings. Do your best.

Life is something to embrace, savor and share and do what we can while we can to leave it better than we found it.

Few knew it or lived it more graciously or courageously than Frank Varischetti Sr.

**So that his place shall never be
with those cold and timid souls
who knew neither victory or defeat.**

Frank died on Aug. 22, 2002. He was 63. At that time, the companies he'd started employed about 1,500 people. His wife Barbara and their four sons – Frank, Steve, Peter and Nick – have continued his legacy of making a difference; by 2019, Varischetti Family enterprises employed more than 10,000 people, including me. I joined Varischetti Holdings, LP in 2014 as Community Initiatives Coordinator.

Open Wide And Say 'Ahhhhhh'

Making a decision and moving on was a defining trait of Dr. Quinn Lundberg Sr., my dentist when I was growing up. His son Quinn Jr. is now the guardian of my mouth.

"That doesn't hurt, does it buddy?"

It's a leading question, but one that Dr. Quinn Lundberg asked me many times as I sat in the chair at his dentist's office in Brockway.

When all was said and done, it never did hurt as much as I feared.

Quinn, who died Saturday, was as decisive and driven as he was generous. His passing will leave a huge hole in the fabric of the community. But his life and work will endure.

When I was a kid, my front teeth decided to grow in, and out, in all directions. An accident with an air rifle chipped one of them, making correcting the situation even more problematic.

Dad and Mom sought the counsel of several specialists on what to do. It took Quinn less than five minutes to answer the question.

One August afternoon in the early 1970s, Quinn filled my gums with Novocain, pulled the offending teeth and

Nick Hoffman

set about fitting me for a partial plate. No debate. No procrastination. He saw what needed to be done and did it. It happened so fast that I didn't have time to get scared.

He never second-guessed that decision. And neither have I.

That was Quinn. Once a course of action became evident, it was full speed ahead.

But he never went so quickly that he left his patients or his friends behind. He always made time for us.

I was in senior high when the time came to extract four impacted wisdom teeth. Back, then, that was a three-day hospital stay. I came home over a weekend and, on Sunday morning, some of my stitches broke. Not pretty.

A call to Quinn and, within hours, after he got home from church as I recall, I was back in his office and the damage was repaired.

That was the rule, not the exception. If you needed him, he was there.

His civic and community involvement knew no bounds and sports was a particular favorite. He was the epitome of a booster and fan.

In recent years, Quinn decided to turn a rolling piece of land off Rattlesnake Road into a golf course. Scottish Heights was born and Quinn was its founder, president and prime mover.

It opened in 1995 and the weather was not its friend. Frequent heavy rains made for tough going and caused serious washout problems, particularly on the 7th hole.

One Saturday that summer, I was standing on the 8th tee. Behind me, a dump truck laden with fill material rumbled down the service road. As the truck passed, Quinn stuck his head out the window, waved and said, "Hi," and moved on to the work at hand.

He could have had someone else do the work. He could

have been playing golf himself. But that wasn't his way. Duty called. And he answered.

Someone told me Quinn rose from a humble background. Given that he was born in the depths of the Great Depression, that would come as no surprise.

His fortunes may have improved, but the humility remained.

Quinn was rich in ways that few people are but in ways to which we can all aspire.

"That doesn't hurt, does it buddy?"

No. Not until Saturday. It will take more than Novocain to soothe that ache.

Doctor, Doctor

Rarely do we look forward to a visit to a doctor's office, but when we need them we're grateful they're there. They can't help but leave an impression, and all the ones who treated me sure did.

The death of Dr. A.E. Devlin of Brockway last week set me to thinking about doctors in general and the many with whom I've dealt in my lifetime.

My first acquaintance with doctors came quite early, at the hands of the late Dr. Nicholas Lorenzo, who delivered me Oct. 22, 1961. He left his mark in two ways: a slight scar on my left cheek from a forceps and my middle name, despite the former. Doc Lorenzo, who also delivered my sister Penny, along with his nurse sidekick, the irrepressible Marge Winterbottom, and saw a lot of another set of my cheeks in my youth, usually with a syringe of penicillin close by.

The elder Dr. Devlin delivered my brother into the world - did such a good job that Kevin's second middle name (Albert) is in honor of Doc Devlin - and his son, Dr. Jim Devlin, ushered our Grandma from it 45 years later.

Nurses Josephine Mooney and, later, Elizabeth Riggle were mainstays of the elder Devlin's practice, from which he retired in 1991. Dr. Devlin and Mrs. Riggle applied the balm and gauze that soothed second-degree burns on my legs, souvenirs from Florida in pursuit of the DuBois Senior Little League All-Stars in 1986.

No matter what ailed me, Doc's wry smile and reassuring manner - and often an envelope of either the green or the pink pills he kept a ready and reliable stock of - did the trick.

When Dr. Jim assumed his father's practice, I was introduced to the concept of the physician assistant and two practitioners, Bill Brown and more recently Casie Burrs, allayed my skepticism and earned my trust and gratitude.

Another caretaker was the scholarly, mild-mannered Dr. James Minteer of Ridgway and his nurse, Mrs. Dolores "Bush" Roth.

Aside from me shoveling food into it, no one has spent more time in my mouth than the father-son tandem of the late Dr. Quinn L. Lundberg Sr. and son Quinn Jr.

Dr. Eric Lundgren, surgeon and son of a surgeon, has attended me several times and, under most urgent circumstances, relied on his instinct and training and rushed Grandma into an operating room and saved her life from a strangulated bowel.

There have been chiropractors, too. The late Harland Adams nursed me through a painful pinched nerve in my neck in the late 1970s and shared tales of working on cadavers from the state penitentiary in Iowa near the Palmer Chiropractic Institute where he studied. He has been followed by Dr. F.G. Salter and, most recently, Dr. Scott Casteel.

Doctors are healers of both body and mind and, for the latter, I have turned to Albert "Buzz" DiGilarmo and Bill Allenbaugh. Seems like it takes lot of doctor-type folks to keep me in one piece.

It takes a lot to be a doctor. Aside from office calls, I didn't pal around with my doctors. I'd see Doc Lorenzo in

Dick Gillung's drug store, waiting for Dick and his clerk, Mrs. Mehall, to lock up so he and Dick could adjourn to the Sportsmen's Club for a few hands of cards. I'd greet Dr. Devlin and his wife, Mary Elizabeth, at the annual Unity Service in Brockway and I invariably bump into Jim Devlin on the sidelines of a Brockway Rover football game, since he's the team physician, plying his trade even in his "off" time.

The more I thought of Dr. Devlin, the more I thought about what doctors surrender when they hang out their shingles. In a world increasingly punctuated by prejudice, vitriol and hatred, doctors don't have the luxury of picking or choosing who they treat when there is an immediate need.

In their eyes, the foulest among us must be given the best care they can provide, the same as they would for you or me. That can't always be easy, but they have a role model, an ancient-of-days healer known as the Great Physician, one whose healing is needed today more than ever.

Most of us have heard of the Hippocratic Oath that doctors take, the one that decrees "do no harm." It says - it commands - more than that.

In part, it reads: "I will prescribe regimens for the good of my patients according to my ability and my judgment and never do harm to anyone. ... I will preserve the purity of my life and my arts. ... In every house where I come I will enter only for the good of my patients ... If I keep this oath faithfully, may I enjoy my life and practice my art, respected by all humanity and in all times ..."

We remember doctors not only for what they do but the nobility and dedication with which they do it. That's how I'll remember Dr. Devlin.

He Was There All the Time

Paw Prints

I grew up surrounded – or more correctly, embraced – by members of the Greatest Generation. Another of their defining traits was the dedication with which they "gave back."

Those paws.

Whenever I think of Floyd Fustine of Brockway, who died Wednesday, I'll think of those paws. Most of us have hands that are proportional to our size. Not Floyd.

Floyd had paws. Big ones, the biggest ones I've ever seen on a human being. It's a good thing God put a set of paws like that on such a gentle man.

And that's the second thing I think of when I think of Floyd, his gentleness and a down-to-earth genuineness and goodness that is all too uncommon in today's culture.

Floyd would have been 91 next month, four days after my Grandmother turns 90. They went to Snyder High School together. She was advanced a grade and caught up to Floyd's class.

In the seven decades since, they've each done their share of living, seen their share of joy and suffering and, like everyone from that era, endured.

Floyd was a U.S. Army veteran of World War II, which surely tested his faith but didn't break it; he was also a member of St. Tobias Church, from where he'll be buried Saturday morning, and where he served as an usher.

Whatever needed doing in the community, Floyd was there: Old Fashioned Fourth of July Committee, volunteer fire company (its oldest member), policeman, mail carrier, bus driver, American Legion member and past commander.

In between, he and his late wife Kathryn raised three daughters and a son.

In his spare time, he liked to play cards, spend time with his friends, root for the Steelers and Pirates and assume his place at Brockway's unofficial monument to its seasoned citizens, the porch at the Brockway Sportsmen's Club.

He seemed to be everywhere, especially when there was a need involved, even if it was a shoulder to cry on or an ear to bend.

Floyd took very little from this life compared to what he gave, and what he leaves behind.

Anyone who knew him won't forget him, especially those paws.

Floyd has found a set of hands bigger than his, the same ones that saw him through 90 years of life.

He and his bearlike paws may be gone, but his fingerprints will remain on Brockway for a long, long time.

'Til The Storm Passes By

That internship in Washington in 1981 changed my mind about a lot of things.

Realizing that each day is a limited, one-time only proposition, never to be repeated, is one of those things. The older I get – and I suspect a lot of folks feel the same way – the more I long to go back and relive some of those days. Sometimes, I do.

It never ceases to amaze me how a long life can be truncated into a handful of vivid recollections, but that's where I find myself in the wake of the death of Grammy Bak.

Those moments involve the resignation of the vice president of the U.S., my learning to ride a bicycle and Christmas.

Maxine Baka, my maternal grandmother, died peacefully Wednesday morning, at home at the age of 84.

Grammy Bak and Pop Bill (her second husband, the late Bill Baka) did a lot of grandparenting of me and my sister Penny and brother Kevin, especially after Dad and Mom divorced in 1972.

One of the neat things about that was that Grammy Bak and Pop Bill liked to eat out. A lot.

We frequented the Dutch Pantry near DuBois, the American Hotel (Interchange) in Brookville and the BP Inn in Brockport.

We were on our way home from the American Hotel on Oct. 10, 1973, when a radio announcer interrupted regular programming to announce that Vice President Spiro T. Agnew had resigned after pleading no contest to income tax evasion. At the time, it seemed like a really big deal.

During the summers of 1973 and 1974, we spent most of our summers at Grammy Bak's and Pop Bill's home on Broad Street in Brockway. That's where I watched a lot of the Watergate hearings and honed my love of politics and public policy.

It was also on Broad Street that I finally learned how to ride a bicycle. I was so overwhelmed at figuring out how to pedal that I forgot to steer - and wiped out a sizable chunk of Grammy Bak's peony plants as I careened into Rittenhouse's yard next door.

It is safe to say that Norman Rockwell wouldn't have made our family his first pick for his portraits but if he had, he could have always relied on us gathering at only one place for Christmas dinner - at Grammy Bak's and Pop Blll's.

I never really thought that much about it. It was just where we went that day, usually about 1 or 2 p.m., whether on Broad Street or later when the scene shifted to Pine Acres in Crenshaw.

As time passed and we grew older - even managing to grow up – we also grew apart.

Pop Bill died in 1991. We "kids," all of her grandchildren, went our separate ways. I don't remember the last time we all got together.

But whatever was going on in our individual lives at the time, Grammy Bak always prepared Christmas dinner for the family.

I sat at the table a few years ago watching Grammy Bak

make her way around the kitchen, overseeing rather that actively participating in the preparation of the feast.

By then, the effects of a number of maladies had begun taking their toll, not on her willingness to keep doing it but rather on her ability to do so.

I realized then what a constant she had been through all those years and trying times, not unlike a lighthouse that provides a reference point to sailors on dark, stormy nights.

Grammy Bak saw her share of storms during her life, too, but now, as the song promises:

When the long night is over,
And the storms come no more
May I stand in Thy presence
On that bright, peaceful shore,
In the land where the tempest
Never comes, Lord, may I
Dwell with Thee
When the storm passes by.

No Such Thing As A Coincidence

I 'll gladly exchange a gallon of fame and fortune for a teaspoon of peace and contentment. And I have found that the things that mean the most are the people I'm sharing the journey with.

One of the beauties of life is that we're never too old to make new friends. Sometimes, when we don't even know we need a friend, God is watching.

This "column" was actually a wedding toast, delivered on Dec. 27, 2008, in my role as best man for Jim Ceriani when he married Heather Gaston.

There are no obvious circumstances that would ever have brought us into contact with each other. Even though some events are cloaked in mystery, nothing in life happens without a reason. I am convinced that there is no such thing as a coincidence.

Yogi Bera, the New York Yankees legendary catcher, is credited with saying, "When you come to a fork in the road, take it."

That's how Jim Ceriani and I met.

I was on my way home from the Courier-Express, where I work(ed) - Jim calls it "play" - as managing editor.

I came to the fork in the road in Brockway, at the Sheetz

store. Going home meant turning right and following Route 219 north.

That night, I was in the mood to drive through town, so I took a left. I saw Nicky Varischetti sitting on the steps in front of the Keith Brothers building. I stopped, sat beside him and the two of us chatted.

An orange car pulled to the curb. A big, strong kid with a smile from ear to ear stepped out and waved. It was Jim, a friend of Nicky's.

After we met, Jim mentioned wanting to find someone to play golf with. I was interested in starting to lift weights, and it was obvious that Jim knew something about that.

And that's how, on a quiet Friday night in July of 2003, we met.

We became good friends very quickly ... that's not hard to do with someone like Jim. We played golf, lifted weights and became best friends.

Two years later, Jim introduced me to Heather and her little girl - now her "big" girl - Alivia. Jim was living in DuBois and when I stopped in after work, if Alivia was there, she'd look up at me, raise her arms and ask me to lift her ... "Uppy," is how she said it.

Jim found out quickly that Heather is a very special woman, and I had an inkling that the two of them had something special going.

A year later, they went on vacation to Florida. The night before they were to come home, my phone rang around 11 o'clock. It was Jim, trying to decide whether to ask Heather to marry him.

Hmmmm, I thought ... no one like a lifelong bachelor to turn to at a time like this, but I'll give it a shot.

"Do you love her?" I asked. "Does she love you like no one else ever has?" The answer to both questions was "yes" and it ended up being one of the shorter conversations we ever had.

A couple days ago, I asked Jim those same two questions. The answer is still "yes."

He left on that trip with an engagement ring in his suitcase. It returned on Heather's finger.

Later that year, we found out that a little boy - a very, very precious little boy - was going to enter the picture. At 9:40 a.m. March 21, 2007, I got a text message from Jim telling me he wanted me to be Cameron's godfather. That message is saved in my cell phone.

Four months later, the phone rang around 4 a.m. Jim and Heather were headed to the hospital. Cameron joined them at 7:31 a.m. Friday, July 27, 2007. The pictures of us all together later that day are saved in my cell phone, too.

Cell phones can store text messages and photos, but none of them can hold all the memories I have since I met Jim ... those are stored in a special place in my heart, where I'll cherish them - along with all the memories we have left to make - all the days of my life.

It doesn't seem possible that all that has happened in five years. But time does not stand still, and God works in mysterious ways, his wonders to perform.

I - we - have been richly blessed.

As with any year, 2008 in particular has seen sorrow tangled with joy and tears mingled with laughter.

Today, as fast away this old year passes, we close it out by adding more joy, laughter and love to the bounty we take from this year, our eyes fixed on the future; our hearts filled with hope.

Fast forward 10 years. Jim and Heather are happily married and living in the Norman Rockwell Americana small town of Smithville, Ohio. Alivia and Cameron are growing up fast and the youngest child, Savannhah

Grace – is racing in her own individualistic way to keep pace.

We don't see each other as often as we'd like. We talk or text a little more frequently. But, as the old saying goes, "Absence makes the heart grow fonder." Amen.

Nick Hoffman

The Curtain Rises,
The Curtain Falls

My godson Cameron played a part in another column
that illustrates the ebb and flow of life.

All the world's a stage,
And all the men and women merely players:
They have their exits and their entrances;
And one man in his time plays many parts.

Those words from Shakespeare's play "As You Like It"
came to mind as I walked along Walburn Run on a summery
spring evening Friday.

I thought about the acts in separate plays that I had
glimpsed that day. They testified to the endless march of
time. The current in Walburn affirmed the notion, its swift
flow pausing in deep pools but always moving, flowing,
fleeting.

The curtain has finally risen on the spring installment of
Nature's four-act play. Buds on trees have become leaves,
green grass has reclaimed the drab aftermath of winter and
prom tuxedos and gowns were the prominent wardrobe in
Brockway Friday evening.

On Friday morning, my godson Cameron Ceriani took

part in the fourth and final play at his preschool class in Ridgway, cast as one of the clowns in the circus-themed performance.

Is it really nearly six years since the curtain went up and I held him in my arms for the first time?

Under the watchful and loving eyes of Dad Jim and Mom Heather, he plays his part on a stage he shares with older sister Alivia, soon to be a third-grader, and younger sister Savannah, whose next big moment comes Thursday when the cast is removed from her broken left leg.

From one adopted family, I moved to the other end of life's stage and paid my respects to the family of Fino Genevro.

He and his leading lady and co-star Flora produced an award-winning testament to love in their 54 years of marriage that produced six children and 19 grand- and great-grandchildren. Not even the final act, which began little more than year ago, dimmed the brilliance of their story.

They welcomed me into their fold nearly 40 years ago and never let me go, holding me close when I needed them most. It was my turn to hold on Friday but, true to form, they again did most of the holding.

It is not easy to watch people you love grieve, but tears of sorrow were indistinguishable from tears of love and joyful remembrance as Flora and the children - Rick, Dave, John, Tommy, Lisa and Anna - formed one prong of an honor guard with brothers Bruno, Frank, Tino, Mario and Geno and sisters Enes, Pena and Irene that greeted hundreds who filed in to pay their respects.

The Genevros are a big family, and a close one. The "family unit" is anything but broken at the homestead along Route 219 in Brockport, not even with the departure of the executive producer and director.

Nick Hoffman

Friday was a day for family. And for plays.

The curtain rises. We play a part; some is scripted, some is improvised as we go along. We make our way to stage right and take one last bow. The curtain falls; intermission begins.

And one man in his time plays many parts.

And the band plays on.

Oh Master, Grant That I ...

Follow the Leader is a kid's game, and not a particularly difficult one as long as there are good leaders. Unfortunately, too many people don't outgrow it, and good leaders are in short supply. That is a lethal combination.

We are horrified when our children's scores on standardized tests fall short of those in other industrialized nations. Why enter, let alone try to win a race to mediocrity? Which one of those other countries ought we trade places with? Why are we doling out "foreign aid?" If their systems are that great, why aren't they paying their own way?

Why does conformity seduce us so? For the same reason the kids my Dad lectured me about jumped off the bridge? Because it's easier to follow than to lead.

America is difficult. Freedom is hard to win and harder to hang onto.

My generation grew up when American Exceptionalism was a reality and the notion of One Nation Under God was indisputable.

No matter what kind of house we want to build, starting out with a solid foundation is essential. So, too, with life.

My Grandmother gave me a good foundation. For a

Nick Hoffman

long time, I knew who Jesus was. But I didn't know Jesus. There's a huge difference. Satan once dwelt in Heaven and knows all too well who Jesus is.

In the polarized environment we live in today, it's easy to forget that the things that unite us are still stronger than the things that we don't agree on. No one demonstrated that to me better than a Catholic clergyman.

People come in all shapes, sizes and with varied talents, all of which play a role in determining how much influence we exert just by entering a room.

Looking back over my acquaintance with the Rev. Msgr. Louis J. Heberlein of St. Tobias Church in Brockway, who died Sunday night, influence is one word that immediately comes to mind.

His presence in a room, particularly the cavernous sanctuary at St. Tobias, could be overwhelming, even intimidating. There was never a doubt that he, in priestly collar or flowing robes, was in charge at the parish he called home for so many years.

Our acquaintance was not always a cordial one.

There was a time when I mistakenly believed that Christian faith involved competition among denominations for the "high holy ground," that one was more right than another.

Given that misconception, and not being of the Catholic faith or fully understanding its tenets, I too often, with malice, denigrated Msgr. Heberlein by not according him the respect his office entitled him to.

He was no shrinking violet but over many years, rather than push me away, he embraced me and played a significant role in melting my bitterness and ignorance. We became friends and established a rapport that continues with his successor, Msgr. Charles Kaza.

Monsignor was, in the best sense of the word, an activist.

He stood up for and advocated what he believed in, even if those views weren't always widely accepted or wildly popular. There was right and there was wrong and the line between them was clear, in his mind's eye.

He possessed a velvet glove and an iron fist, and could use them with equal aplomb.

Right makes might, and the self-assurance that he was right gave Monsignor an imposing presence.

He presided at the funerals of some of my family members and many of my friends.

Secreted in a back pew at St. Tobias, I could remain out of the way and not interfere with the celebration of the sacraments attendant the Mass.

I could also weep as the homily gave way to Communion, the last good-bye and the recessional from the sanctuary.

Monsignor's most powerful feature was a rich, deep voice.

As he cast incense and offered the final prayer, he would instruct those in attendance to join him in the last hymn, which usually came down to "How Great Thou Art," "The Prayer of St. Francis" or "Come to His Aid."

The Prayer of St. Francis has always been special to me. Monsignor never failed to reach down deep into my soul and reduce me to unabashed tears as he concluded the Mass. The tone of his voice punctuated each syllable of the song's climax:

"Oh, Master, grant that I may never seek
"So much to be consoled as to console
"To be understood as to understand
"To be loved as to love with all my soul."

Occasionally, while I drive down the road (with the windows up, of course), I'll try my hand at imitating those words in that tone. It isn't the same, but I imagine he'd smile if he heard me try ... and leave little doubt that imitation, no matter how sincere, is not always flattering.

He endured a debilitating disease in his final years, one I suspect feared him much more than he feared it.

For a time, I was aware only that our lives followed different paths. Knowing him revealed that our paths were forks on the same road.

Grant him eternal rest, O Lord.

More Work To Do

A friend of my Dad's made a powerful impression from a situation that is often looked upon as a defeat ... except for those who know that "faith is the victory."

Legacies are the glue that connects past, present and future. They add continuity to life and pass, often unnoticed, from decade to decade and generation to generation.

In September, the renewal of one legacy and the birth of another began when my Dad returned home to celebrate his mother's 80th birthday.

Part of the celebration included the baptism of my sister's son, my godson, Caden.

The baptism took place at Terry Felt's Beechtree Union Church. I'd worshipped there with my grandmother, as a pre-teen, back when Terry's dad, the late George Felt, was in the pulpit.

The baptism reacquainted my dad with an old, dear friend of his, Dale "Cuffy" Carnahan.

In the 1960s and early '70s, before my Dad left Brockway, he and Cuffy and a pack of their friends spent a lot of time together, centered at the Timber Lanes bowling alley, which Dad managed.

There are pictures of Cuffy and his wife, Charlotte, and other couples in our house. There are also bowling trophies, including the 1967 Coca Cola Traveling Trio League that they - Dad, Cuffy and Fred Blakney, the "Gems," captured.

I knew who Cuffy was but, once Dad left, our paths didn't cross very much. Until that Sunday in church.

Before Dad and his wife Fran went back to Omaha, Cuffy paid a visit and he and Dad spent hours reminiscing, talking and reaffirming their friendship.

My grandma and I continued to attend Beechtree and each Sunday, Cuffy extended us a warm greeting.

Earlier this year, tests revealed that Cuffy was ill. The prognosis wasn't encouraging. The last time we saw him in church, that tall, husky, humble, loving giant of a man hugged us both and we cried, as many did that day.

Cuffy's faith in his Lord was a living and powerful force, one that even the shadow of death couldn't and didn't dim.

My Dad passed on the legacy of friendship with Cuffy, as he's done with many of his contemporaries, admitting me into special bonds that remain intact despite many miles and years.

I visited Cuffy one Friday morning not long ago. Any consolation I could give him paled in the comfort he gave me. As I prepared to leave, he suggested we pray.

I grasped his hand and bowed my head as my friend and my Dad's friend prayed, not for himself, not for his life, but for mine.

He knew I'd encountered some bumps in recent years and that other obstacles left, as he said, "more work to do."

He knew for a certainty that his future was secure. His prayer was that mine would be, too.

And so a birthday and a baptism opened the door to a legacy from my Dad, one that paved the way for a legacy from Cuffy.

Sometimes, the lights that burn brightest dim quickly. But the warmth of their glow can last much longer.

So it is with Cuffy, who died Sunday.

His Silence Was Deafening

In each of our lives, there are turning points and moments of truth – decisions we make or actions we take – or don't - that affect and even define our destiny. Some are crystal clear and unmistakable when they happen. Others are more subtle.

By the time I reached 30, I was for the most part on top of the world – and at the same time, was hurtling out of control to a crash landing.

Anytime you have to ask if you have a problem, you probably do. I did. I knew something was wrong in 1986 and was so distraught that I checked myself into the detoxification unit in DuBois.

Three days later the doctors, unable to document any physical manifestations of addiction, gave me a clean bill of health. Great, I thought, and celebrated by getting drunk that night.

A year later, I was arrested for my first DUI. Stunned, I quit drinking for seven months. I even wrote a column about the experience. Time dulled my senses. I was OK, right? Those doctors said so.

Over Labor Day weekend, we had a tournament at the golf course. And a keg of beer. A couple cold ones couldn't hurt, could they?

Fast forward five years. I was an alcoholic, and had

been since my college days. I didn't admit it, but deep down I feared I was. Others had noticed, too, and one of them got my attention in a way I've never forgotten.

There are several words that come to mind when I think of Jack Biss, and the one that says it best is "gentleman."

When you come from a small town like Brockway, Jack is one of the "legacy" presences in your life. He and my Dad played Little League baseball when it began in Brockway in 1950. Dad was 12; Jack was 11. Dad hit the first home run in Brockway LL. Jack was a pitcher who, because of his size, could "bring it" so hard and fast that he only played one year; his father feared he might hurt someone if one of his pitches got away from him.

That's how I "inherited" Jack from my Dad's generation, the same way I inherited Bud and Jean Grieneisen, because Dad was Bud's best man when he married Jean on Oct. 22, 1955 (the date sticks in my head because, six years later, it became my birthday).

Jack's Men's Shop was a fixture on Main Street when I was growing up, bookended by two of my favorite shops on the 300 block – Brockway Drug Co. and Moody's Variety Store, which added up to two of the three best candy counters a kid could wish for (the other was Gillung's Pharmacy, directly across the street).

My Grandmother participated in one of Jack's special offers in which purchases earned the buyer bonus points that could be saved up for future purchases. After Dad and Mom divorced in 1972, Dad moved west to Denver and later to Omaha. Grandma saved up her points to buy him dress shirts from time to time and even a men's suit.

When Grandma died in 2010, she still had points "on the books" at Jack's, which by then was located on Brady Street in DuBois. No one but Jack could have known about those points but, always the gentleman, he gave me those points and I bought a couple of dress shirts.

Jack was an avid golfer and I a budding one back in the days when merchants and bankers closed up shop at noon on Wednesdays to hit the links. Jack and I didn't get to play together often, but I remember very well one of those occasions. Brockway Glass Golf Course hosted a Firecracker Open as part of Brockway's Old-Fashioned Fourth of July celebration in the days when Perk Binney was running the pro shop.

Jack and I were in the 2nd Flight and ended up playing together in the tournament in the late 1970s or early 1980s. He was the better player but I played way over my head on the front nine and shot 40, which included ricocheting my second shot off a rock in the creek in front of the 9th green and onto the green. I missed the ensuing birdie putt but shot 40, and built a big lead going into the back 9.

I didn't do anything stupid ... until we got to the last hole, No. 9 the second time. I had 38 strokes through 8 holes, and a par would give me an 82, my best score ever to that point. The magic disappeared and I choked the whole way to the house and by the time the bloodshed ended, I had taken a quadruple-bogey 8, a snowman, and my visions of grandeur evaporated before my eyes. I managed to hold on for a 2-shot win over Mr. Biss, who was gracious as always.

My most poignant memory, the one I'll never forget, came several years later when I was in the throes of the alcoholic haze I spent the Lost Decade of my 20s in. I was at the Rocky Grill in Brockway. In those days, diners had to come to the bar area to pay their bill.

Jack was leaning against the corner of the bar while he waited to pay his bill. My back was to him, and he wasn't looking when I turned around. His head was shaking side to side and he had a mournful look in his eyes. He didn't say a word, but I heard him loud and clear: "What a shame."

That image has stuck with me for the better part of 30 years. Its effect wasn't immediate, but it has been long-lasting; it hurt to think that I had let Mr. Biss down and disappointed him.

Years later, not long before he and his wife Pat retired from the clothing business, I shared that incident with Jack. And I thanked him. I'll always be grateful to that gentle man, that gentleman, for doing more than he could imagine to help me get back on track. Like they say, "That's what friends are for."

Collision Course

I was failing my family, my friends, my job and everything that mattered, or should matter, in a person's life.

It was 1992 and my cup was running over ... with booze.

By the end of that year, my cup would be running over with a far more intoxicating brew, one of love and compassion and redemption. Between the two extremes lay a long and winding road.

I was in trouble at work, either from showing up less than able to work, or not showing up at all. I'd been encouraged to get my act together ... and told in no uncertain terms that I was expendable.

On more than one occasion, I had to hold a mug of beer with both of my shaking hands to get it to my lips.

One night during those dark years, I had a dream that featured a calm but firm voice, "I made you for better than this." That was it; no lightning, no earthquake, no angels swirling around my bed. I kept drinking, ... but I couldn't shake that dream or those words.

My season of reckoning began on a Saturday night. Feb. 1, 1992. As usual on weekends in those days, I embarked on a daylong binge, fell asleep at a bar and capped things off by getting behind the wheel in a semiconscious haze. This time wasn't going to end "as usual," however.

I rear-ended a car on the way home. No damage, no injuries. I vaguely remember the driver getting in my face, but I left the scene, drove home and went to bed, content that I'd skated by again.

Then the police showed up, arrested and handcuffed me and took me to the station. My blood alcohol content was 0.278 percent – 3 ½ times the legal limit. No one gets to that level of intoxication without drinking regularly and heavily.

I lashed out, blaming anyone and everyone I could think of. Except me.

"They're messing with the wrong guy," I screamed when I returned home. "They'll pay dearly for this!"

I hired an attorney and launched an all-out assault on this travesty of justice. While there were some legitimate questions about the process that resulted in my arrest, District Justice Bernard "Tink" Hetrick found enough evidence to send the matter to the county court.

This was my second DUI offense, the first having come in 1987. If I was found guilty this time, I'd be looking at 30 days in jail, thousands of dollars in fines and costs, losing my driver's license for a year and, probably, my job.

I invested several thousand dollars to fight the charges. When the meter is running, the wheels of justice seem to grind to a halt. Legal briefs, answers, motions, more briefs.

A few months later, I called my attorney, Jeff Gordon, to get an update on the case. That's when lightning flashed.

"Nick, do you have a problem?" he asked.

Blindsided by the question and with my deflector shields down, my answer was brief and honest. "Yes," I said.

District Attorney Mark Wallisch, Chief Probation Officer Larry Straitiff and the prosecuting officer had agreed to offer me a plea agreement that would substitute a 30-day inpatient alcohol rehabilitation program for the jail term. I asked Jeff to find out if the offer was still on the table. It was. I took it.

I entered my plea before Judge William L. Henry in mid-July. But the madness didn't stop. I kept drinking, every night. My world revolved around my drinking time. Nothing could or would interfere.

During that spring, I had moved in with Nan at Dad's urging.

Nan had a franchise with God and Jesus Christ; together they made a business of salvaging lost souls. I was to become one of their projects.

But not just yet.

Unable to imagine or endure life without liquor, I tried to drink it all before I stood before Judge Henry again.

Despondent and frightened, I entertained unimaginable thoughts of killing myself and made one less than enthusiastic attempt to do so. A very good friend brought me back from the edge and told me to shape up.

I was slowly coming to realize how much trouble I was really in and how much help I needed. I wanted Dad to be a part of whatever lay ahead.

That's when he made the call to the referral line and we learned about Valley Hope in Norton, Kan.

Would the court system allow me to travel, unescorted, halfway across the country? Maybe not, but we wouldn't know until we tried.

Psychologist Bill Allenbaugh did evaluations of DUI defendants at the time. I had to convince him that I was worth the risk. Our paths had crossed once before. I didn't remember him. But he remembered me.

Remember when I checked into the detox unit in 1986 when I thought I had a problem? Bill was called in to consult with the doctors. He interviewed me. He remembers the conversation better than I. He told me I didn't want anything to do with counseling or help. Bill made a mental note to himself, "I'll see him again."

"Again" was here.

Bill decided I was worth trying to save and Valley Hope seemed to be my last best hope. He and the others signed off and I was on my way to Kansas.

I was scheduled to appear before Judge Henry at 10:30 a.m. Wednesday, Sept. 16, 1992. After I finished work on the 15th, I headed for the bars one last time.

Near 2 a.m., I swallowed the last gulp of my last glass of Budweiser. Eight hours later, even though I couldn't have passed a breathalyzer test, I stood before Judge Henry, who agreed to the terms of the plea agreement, sentenced me to go to Kansas and wished me well.

He didn't notice but one of the probation officers recognized the aroma of booze about me. He told me that would be the last and only time he'd let it go.

I was about to enter completely uncharted territory. My life was hanging in the balance.

Let Go And Let God

On Saturday, Sept. 19, I flew to Omaha. On Monday, Dad and his wife, Fran, whom I called and still call Mom, and I set off for Norton, Kan., 280 miles west of Omaha.

Norton isn't a lockdown, hospital-type treatment center. It's an old motel that's been converted into one of the top rehab programs in the nation.

After I checked in, we went to the chapel.

There are moments in life when time stands still, when an unseen power allows us to catch our breath and get our bearings. This was my time.

We knelt and prayed. More precisely, we begged and wept and pleaded that whatever it took for me to get sober, whatever it was that I didn't have, that God would grant it, give me back my life and give me back to those who loved me.

Over the next month, the miracle happened. I didn't drink. I didn't want to drink. I wanted to live. I wanted to love. I learned to love myself. I learned that I have - just like anyone else and everyone else - unique talents and abilities that can make the world a better place. And each of us has an obligation to do exactly that.

In "It's a Wonderful Life," George Bailey is given a glimpse of what the world would have been like if he had not been born. The cold reality of how much we mean to each other begins to sink in. That's when Clarence, his guardian angel, says, "Strange, isn't it? Each man's life touches so many other lives. When he isn't around he leaves an awful hole, doesn't he?"

Thirty days later, on my 31st birthday, Oct. 22, I left Norton and began the rest of My Wonderful Life, praying that I, like George Bailey, could brighten the little corner of the world I'm lucky enough to inhabit.

I didn't leave the writer behind while I was in rehab. I knew that this was my last shot to get sober. Win or lose, I wanted to have a record of the experience. I kept a journal. Five years later, I submitted a column to Valley Hope's "Coffee Cup" newsletter, that included these excerpts from that journal.

9/21/92

After only eight hours here, I'm sure of two things already – there is no way this experience is not going to make me a better person, and the next time I start feeling sorry for the "hand that I've been dealt," I hope God or somebody down here gives me a good swift kick.

The answers I need are here. I only hope that I have the courage to seek them and to be able to face whatever I find.

9/22/92

I was on the verge of tears at least a dozen times today as feelings of ecstasy, hate, fear, frustration and most of all, hope, flooded my soul.

Am I so afraid of being hurt? Apparently I am. That is going to be the cornerstone of my recovery – learning to love myself and, in turn, learning to love others. I know that I have

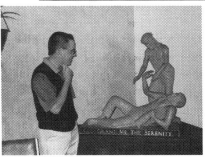

Miracle at Valley Hope, from top-Talking with
patients; a sober reminder; there is Hope; Nick with
Dad, Mom and Nan; Nick & his counselor.

Nick Hoffman

the capacity to do so. That's why I think I nearly cried so many times today. There's a wonderful, positive loving person waiting to burst forth and blossom. He will, too. I'm sure.

9-23-92

I staged a big comeback and beat Ken C. in a 1,000-point game of rummy. He could have won easily but he made some dumb pick-ups. I think he lives life the same way – he knows he has what it takes to win, but he loses interest and ends up losing. He can always say the system beat him ... quite a complex person.

9-29-92

I'm stubborn, angry and very introverted. My counselor told me that I was/am predisposed to alcoholism or some form of addiction. When I drank for the first time in 1978, the die was cast. It's too late to change the past, but it's obvious that if I ever drink again, I'll be right back to where I was - or worse - in no time.

10-1-92

It's ironic that as I come to realize I have to give more of myself, more than just words, that this chance (a nomination to the United Way board back home) comes along ... I've taken a lot from life for a lot of wrong reasons. It's time to start giving back for the right reasons.

10-6-92

I feel great about the program so far and I hope the next three days open a lot more opportunities for honesty, forgiveness and sharing. I'm not such a bad guy after all.

10-7-92

I'm going to let go of all the past. I won't forget it, but it's not an excuse for anything anymore. They were experiences that shaped me and taught me and that's how I want to remember them – that somehow, I'm better for them.

10-9-92

I've felt an inner peace and patience for the last several days. I'm not as conscious of worry or anxiety. It feels good ... I can't remember feeling this at ease. Nothing seems to be a pressing, urgent worry ... as Bob (Valley Hope chaplain) said in a lecture today, and something I've forgotten for too long: "God help me to remember that nothing is going to happen today that you and I can't handle together."

10-14-92

I did my discharge testing – what a difference! I feel better and think differently and I'm at peace. God does work miracles! The feelings are indescribable!

10-20-92

The group surprised me with a birthday cake and card tonight. Ken M. let them know – their love touches me deeply. I damn near cried three times today, saying "so

Nick Hoffman

long" will be tough. It's like leaving home, leaving family. They've touched me, loved me and helped me to find myself! They're very special. I'll miss them. Again, words fail me. There just aren't words that can capture the peace, serenity and love that I feel.

Thirty days ago, I wrote that the answers I needed were here if I'd work hard and be honest. They were and I found them. George Bailey lives and miracles do happen on Christmas Eve in Bedford Falls, and on my birthday in Norton, Kansas. Thank you God for bringing my journey through Norton and Valley Hope. It's a Wonderful Life.

Have You Got The Spirit?

During my annual trips to Omaha to visit my Dad, he and I returned to Valley Hope and Norton almost every year for the 25 years after I was in treatment.

While I was a patient, "alumni" occasionally stopped in to tell their story of recovery. At first, I thought they came to "rub our noses in it" and show off. But I learned that the best way to sell a product is to tout its successes.

I eventually realized that I had an obligation to share my story in hope of inspiring those who sat where I once did, wondering if their lives could be salvaged.

I shared a lot of hugs in the ensuing 25 years and I never felt that that trip was a waste of time. I looked forward to it. It rejuvenated me. Dad and I thrived on it. I started taking the "scenic route" instead of Interstate 80 in order to enjoy the ride, visit the bucolic little towns that dot the Plains and enjoy the "wide open" spaces that, for me, whispered "freedom" in my ear.

My counselor at Valley Hope had a reputation as being tough, something many of the patients feared. But we hit it off and neither of us held anything back.

After my visit in 2003, my counselor wrote a piece for Valley Hope's "Coffee Cup" newsletter.

"Whenever I hear Nick talk about his spiritual life,

I can only smile at the wonder of it a when I remember how far down he had fallen when he came to treatment 11 years ago. Nick carries the message of spiritual recovery wherever he is. He is a very observant child of God. I have never heard Nick claim that 'religion' is where it's at. He has always talked about 'Spirituality." I appreciate that.

"My personal experiences with religion have not been very productive. ... I am a Christian ... I do have a personal relationship with my Higher Power whom I call God. It has worked for me for a very long time. He has taught me a great deal about my world and has given me the strength to work through my own issues as they arise. We talk and walk together daily. Sometimes I don't listen very well and he lets me know it by letting things go the way I think I want them and when they fall apart we get together again and I start listening.

"To me that is the big difference between religion and spirituality. Religion gets in the way of spirituality in my opinion. I can't hear what God wants me to hear when I am listening to someone tell me that all will be well as long as I 'bring it to the cross.' Things are not always going to 'be well' and I need to know what is expected of me when I get into trouble and how I am to behave when things are going well.

"Religion doesn't teach me that. Nick has the right idea. Find God where you are, no matter where that is; on a Kansas/Nebraska prairie, a jail cell or an office on the 50th floor of some high rise, or in a hospital room with someone who is taking their last breath. God will lead us if we are open and trusting that things will 'be well' with time and with some **effort** on our part. That is the effort it takes to **be** with God. God's love is expressed in the way we treat others and the way we respond when others *don't treat us well. We grow from it all and get what they call 'character.' Sometimes I think I have enough but often I find a little more character coming my way. A friend of mine in recovery said it well: 'I never had a bad day in recovery. I have good days and growing days.' How could it be said any better?'"*

Nick Hoffman

That Saved A Wretch Like Me

Norton is never very far away. I was reminded of that at a church service in 2013.

"Twas grace that taught my heart to fear, and grace those fears relieved."

That's as far as I got in the second verse of "Amazing Grace" as we closed a Sunday service at Beechtree Union Church near Brockway recently.

"Amazing Grace" - No. 343 in our hymnal - is one of a handful of songs I don't need the book for. The words are etched in my brain, and seared in my soul.

Pastor Terry Felt and I talked about the song before the service started that Sunday.

Did I know the history of it? Yes, I know.

The song was written by John Newton who, of all things, was the captain of a slave ship in the 18th century, bringing kidnapped Negros to the Colonies for a life of servitude to white aristocrats in the South.

Amazing grace, how sweet the sound
That saved a wretch like me
I once was lost, but now am found;
Was blind, but now I see.

The theory is that the slaves in the hold of Newton's ship chanted the melody to a sorrow chant. Indeed, while Newton is credited with the words, the melody of "Amazing Grace" is officially listed as "unknown."

In 1748, on one of his voyages, Newton's life changed forever. One version records it thus:

"The ship encountered a severe storm off the coast of Donegal and almost sank. Newton awoke in the middle of the night and finally called out to God as the ship filled with water.

"After he called out, the cargo came out and stopped up the hole, and the ship was able to drift to safety. It was this experience which he later marked as the beginnings of his conversion to evangelical Christianity. As the ship sailed home, Newton began to read the Bible and other religious literature.

"By the time he reached Britain, he had accepted the doctrines of evangelical Christianity. The date was 10 May 1748, an anniversary he marked for the rest of his life."

> *Twas grace that taught my heart to fear*
> *And grace my fears relieved*
> *How precious did that grace appear*
> *The hour I first believed*

The song was part of the miracle that is my life in the autumn of 1992.

At age 30, I was in alcohol rehab at Valley Hope in Norton, Kan., one of 40-some broken souls looking for our last best hope for something other than certain death.

A group of us congregated outside one night. Ken, fresh from a state prison stretch for armed robbery. A young woman facing manslaughter charges in Missouri for the stabbing death of her brother in a drug deal gone bad. And Leon, a drug addict who, along with his wife, were looking for their miracle.

Someone started humming the tune. Most of us knew the first verse and joined in. We stumbled into the second verse and reverted to humming the melody.

The Lord has promised good to me
His word my hope secures
He will my shield and portion be
As long as life endures.

That verse is the "contract language" of the song.

As attorneys Ed Ferraro and Dave King drilled into my head in my youth as I toyed with becoming a lawyer, basic contract law consists of an offer, acceptance and consideration.

The third verse fills that formula - "has promised," "secures," "He will" and "as long as."

Simple. Miraculous.

Through many dangers, toils and snares
I have already come
'Tis grace hath brought me safe this far
And grace will lead me home.

As the second verse began that Sunday at Beechtree, tears began streaming down my cheeks. My voice choked. I was transported back to that night with the group at Valley Hope.

It was overlaid with those slaves in the hold of John Newton's ship. Enslaved in dark places of our making, we sang the words to the melody they - enslaved through no choice of their own - chanted, centuries and worlds apart, all longing for something that seemed beyond our comprehension or grasp.

I don't know how many of us held on to the grace we found on the plains of Kansas during our stays at Valley Hope. By God's amazing grace, I have. Twenty-one years and counting, one day at a time.

When we'd been there 10,000 years
Bright shining as the sun
We've no less days to sing God's praise
Than when we'd first begun.

Nick Hoffman

It's In The Cards

As I neared the end of my stay at Valley Hope and began thinking about the rest of my life, I was acutely aware that I would have a lot of time to fill in, especially since I wouldn't have a driver's license for one year.

By Thanksgiving of 1992, I was right back where I started – in the house that Pa Segers built, the house I grew up in. It welcomed me back and provided sanctuary when things at home blew up in 1975. Now, it beckoned again, offering the sanctuary I so badly needed and a time to heal.

As I hoped, Dad and Mom were able to be there for my stay at Norton. They spent a couple weekends there to lend their support to my rehabilitation effort.

Mom gave me a token on which were inscribed words that anyone can live by ... and one alcoholics like me must always remember:

> *God grant me the serenity*
> *To accept the things I cannot change*
> *Courage to change the things I can*
> *And the wisdom to know the difference.*

Their presence meant so much, and I'll love them both forever.

Now, it was Nan's turn. And as she always had - and always would – she "tended to me." I had invested in preserving the house and reconditioning it. Nan invested in my recovery and provided all I needed.

She drove me to and from work for a year – got me there in time to start at 2 p.m. and was waiting every night at 11 o'clock when it was time to go home.

All my needs were met, including the most important one – the spiritual aspect. When we were growing up, she gathered me and my siblings and a couple of neighborhood kids around the kitchen table each morning for devotions while we waited for the school bus.

In my post-recovery world, I became acutely aware of the necessity of thankfulness. It is too easy to focus on what's going wrong rather than what is going right or of what we don't have instead of what we do.

I made up a list of people I'd send Christmas cards to. They included many of those you've been reading about. The list grew ... and grew ... until it exceeded 200. This year (2019) it's near 300.

Nan and I ordered a Christian tract to include with the cards. "The Touch of the Master's Hand" or "The Night Before Jesus Came" were among the titles.

I wrote a greeting in each card and addressed the envelope. Nan "stuffed" the tract into the card and affixed the stamp and return label to the envelope. It must have looked like Santa's workshop.

Each year, around Thanksgiving, we'd start "the cards." We learned to pace ourselves so it didn't become work, so that we could spend time thinking about each person and what they meant to us. Each card was signed **Nick and Nan**

We sold the house in 2006. Nan died in 2010. But the tradition lives on.

Last Thursday got off to a rough start.

It snowed, roads were tricky and waves of more bad economic news crashed ashore. Stock markets were plunging and analysts were warning of worse days ahead. Fear was in full bloom and panic seemed to be right around the corner.

I was home, using up some vacation days.

"Enough!" I said. I hit "mute" on my TV, put on a Christmas carols CD and went to the dining room table to resume whittling away at my Christmas card list.

The names on Page 4 included former Brockway police Chief Bob Stowman. We endured some rocky moments when I was growing up and Bob taught me some tough lessons. I'm still grateful.

Bonnie Siple was one of my high school teachers, one who left her indelible imprint on my education, and life. She and her husband Glenn worship at the same old country church – Beechtree Union – that I attend each week.

Pastor Terry Felt and his wife Sylvia enrich my life each week at Beechtree, but I haven't forgotten the night, many years ago, that then Snyder Township police Chief Felt apprehended me for underage drinking. I was a little slower to realize how lucky I was that night.

Msgr. Charles Kaza of St. Tobias Church in Brockway has furthered the work his predecessor, Msgr. Louis Heberlein, began in helping a bitter young man realize that faith is about more than denominations. We worship the same God, just in different places and in different ways. I cherish his friendship, and the faith we share.

The staff at the Valley Hope treatment center in Norton, Kan., and my counselor while I was in alcohol rehab in 1992 will always have a very special place in my heart. One day at a time, my visit to Norton each year is a journey I look forward to.

Ann and Gary Cristini have been friends and supporters for a long time, even though Ann and I crossed swords a few times when she was Brockway's mayor. I've grown a lot since then.

Dave Benson, retired Brockway postmaster, made sure my Christmas cards were delivered in his region, even after 911 addressing rendered RDs obsolete and some area postmasters refused to deliver them.

The list goes on.

Each person on that page – and the other pages of the list - brightened my life, made me a better person, shared sorrow, celebrated triumph, rooted for me, prayed for me.

Take away any one of them and the mosaic of my life isn't as bright.

An hour after I started, I took a break and looked outside.

It had stopped snowing. The sun had broken through the clouds and patches of blue brightened the sky. The stock market had regained more than 200 points.

It will snow again, and clouds will blot out the sun. Others can worry about what the markets do; the Dow ended up plunging 445 points that day.

The world didn't change in that hour last Thursday morning. But the way I chose to look at it did.

The experiment worked again; when we focus on being thankful, fear is revealed as the great imposter it is.

As much as there is to be concerned about this Thanksgiving, there is much more to be thankful for.

Stock market rallies and routs, meltdowns, bailouts, presidents and politicians come and go. They have their roles but they can only do so much and none of them lasts forever.

The rest – and what matters most - is up to us. Fear and panic on one hand, thanksgiving and hope on the other.

Who's next on my Christmas card list?

Nick Hoffman

In 2018, the Tract League in Grand Rapids, Mich., announced it would stop selling tracts in the U.S. due to declining sales in order to focus its efforts in India, where there is great demand.

Someday, I won't be able to find the Christian-themed Christmas cards in boxes of 36 or 32 at Dollar General or Wal-Mart.

If they don't disappear completely, Christmas cards will be exclusively digital, before they become passé, much like visits to cemeteries on Memorial Day have become.

But as long as I live, I'll remember all these folks and more. Who would I be without them? I'll borrow the words of New York Yankees great Lou Gehrig: "Today, I consider myself the luckiest man on the face of the earth."

Grandma Goes Dumpster Diving

Nan and I had a lot of fun in the 15 years we lived at the "manor" until its sale in 2006. The times we shared could fill a separate book.

She found Jesus Christ at a camp meeting in Brockway when she was 13 or 14 years old. In the middle of the Great Depression, her father's sister, Aunt Marie and her husband Jim offered to take Nan from the poverty she grew up in and exchange it for life in the lap of luxury.

She tried it but soon recognized that it wasn't her calling. Nan turned her back on riches and comfort and spent the rest of her life doing God's work and introducing anyone she came in contact with to "My Jesus."

When she was involved in a minor fender-bender in DuBois, the police officer who responded to the scene asked her if she was alone in her car when the mishap occurred. "No, I wasn't," she told him. "Who was with you?" the officer asked. "My Jesus," she answered.

When people like Nan have such a positive and enduring impact on our lives, they're not gone when they die as much as they are absent.

I tried to express that thought when she died in 2010.

If you asked my Grandmother, Jo Hoffman, "How are you?" she'd no doubt reply, "I'm just fine."

Even when she wasn't, she said she was.

When she died Sept. 17, one week short of her 91st birthday, she didn't leave me gold or silver, stocks, bonds, land or jewels. Those would be spent or lose their value.

"I'm just fine" is my inheritance, along with the faith in a living God and a risen Savior that is its foundation.

You're my peace of mind
in this crazy world.
You're everything I've tried to find,
your love is a pearl.
You're my Mona Lisa,
you're my rainbow skies,
and my only prayer
is that you realize
you'll always be
beautiful in my eyes.

Shortly after the time came to sell our family homestead four years ago, for me to go my way and Nan to go to Toby Terrace, something happened that capsulizes what she was all about.

Each day, she'd take a small bag of trash to the dumpster behind Building C. She told me about "rescuing" a lamp from the dumpster. Such a pretty lamp it was. It didn't work anymore, but it was too pretty to throw away.

I shared the story with Dad and we recoiled in mock terror at the thought of the sight of Nan, clad in her tattered flannel pajamas - which she refused to replace with one of countless new pairs that filled a dresser drawer - diving through a dumpster in search of salvageables.

There's a reason that lamp was in the dumpster - it didn't work anymore. Lamps are mass produced and are intended to wear out. If they don't, the people who make them go out of business.

People are different. Each one is unique. And each one is worth trying to save.

How fitting that the woman who spent most of her life diving into the dumpster of life's discards would find beauty and value in a cast-off lamp.

She believed with all her heart that every person God made had value and worth and could be redeemed, could be salvaged, could be made to work again. Her legacy is one of human reclamation projects, lifting up many people who had been disposed of by the noisy crowd. She never gave up on them because God never gave up on her and, knowing His love and grace, she knew that nothing is impossible.

I am living proof of someone reclaimed from life's dumpster. Only God knows for sure how many hours she prayed for me and how many prayers she offered up for my redemption, safety and salvation. And I am only one.

She gave breath to the notion that life's simple pleasures are the best ... a trip to the Tastee Freez, a walk up Walburn Run, mowing the grass, meditating each morning with Jesus, a cup of tea and a bowl of rolled oats, taking a ride through Munderf and Richardsville and all points in between to view the splendor of the autumn foliage, sitting in her rocking chair and reading her Bible then falling asleep to bask in the peace and serenity she found in her Lord, Jesus Christ.

The last ride came Sept. 21, a funeral procession to Temple Cemetery. She'd have gloried in that day ... crystal blue skies, brilliant sunshine, dazzling fall colors. And I have no doubt that she did revel in it with us, even if from afar.

Nick Hoffman

*The world will turn
and the seasons will change,
and all the lessons we will learn
will be beautiful and strange.
We'll have our fill of tears,
our share of sighs.
And my only prayer
is that you realize
you'll always be beautiful
in my eyes.*

She cared for her mother for years, and was at her bedside in 1973, telling her it was OK to let go and go home. Her mother took a deep breath, sighed and slipped away. I whispered those words to Nan when I left her room the night of Sept. 16. A few hours later, the phone rang and I got the news that the Great Conductor had, at last, given the "All aboard!" call for her trip home.

She cared for her father until the night he died in 1980, having told no one, including him, that he was dying of cancer.

Day after day, she went to him in the morning, fed him and cared for him, then went home to care for her husband, who was recovering from a heart attack. She went back to Grandpa's at lunchtime then back home then back again for his evening meal.

Nan

Nick Hoffman

The only day he spent in the hospital was the day he died. She fixed his oats that morning. He took one bite, pushed the bowl aside and said, "I'll eat the rest later." He died that night.

Five months later, she was with her husband in an ambulance on the way to Pittsburgh; he died in Kittanning. And she was with Wee Wee when he died in 1993.

Four of the most important and beloved people in her life, and she was the one who shepherded them from this life into the next. I imagine that God scoured the halls of Heaven to find an angel suitable to the task, then realized he had one already here. And, as with all the tasks He gave her, she carried them out with love and devotion.

When there are lines upon my face
from a lifetime of smiles,
and when the time comes to embrace
for one long last while,
we can laugh about
how time really flies.
We won't say goodbye
'cause true love never dies.
You'll always be beautiful in my eyes.

As important as it is for each of us to ask who saved us from the dumpster of life, the more pressing question is who will we lift up, to whom will we offer her Jesus as she offered Him to us.

Each and every person, without exception, is designed to be a player in God's grand symphony orchestra. We are the notes of his Opus. Someday, we'll gather together and play that Opus in an avalanche of love and harmony and praise the likes of which has never been seen or heard.

She's there, waiting. And she's just fine.

**You will always be
beautiful in my eyes.
And the passing years will show
that you will always grow
ever more beautiful in my eyes.**

Nick Hoffman

An Empty Seat, But I'm Not Alone

I think of Nan often, no more so than on my first Thanksgiving without her.

This will be the 50th Thanksgiving of my lifetime ... and the first without my Grandmother.

From the time the leaves changed color each year until we shared a Christmas Eve candlelight service at Beechtree Union Church in Westville, this time of the year is as good as life can be.

Walks along Walburn Run, whether braced against chill winds or bathed in Indian Summer sunshine; Sunday afternoons after church ensconced in our ancestral home in its engulfing warmth; the smell of coffee brewing woven with the aroma of blueberry muffins in the oven; a ride through the country to marvel at the foliage; putting up the Christmas tree in the dead of night while she slept, a role reversal from the nights she labored with presents and baking while visions of sugar plums danced in my head as a youth.

Moments like those punctuated our lives. We yearned and gave thanks for them.

Through those years, as she made her way through her 70s and 80s, she marveled that she'd been blessed with the gift of years. She knew the end of that road, like the end of Walburn Run, lay somewhere ahead.

She was not one to fear that proverbial end of the road. As the 80s became 90, she embraced the notion that each day was one step closer to a long-awaited meeting with "my Jesus."

From time to time, she'd probe to determine if I was as prepared as she, chiding me kiddingly for "not listening to anything I say."

But I did hear. And I listened. And I knew.

Even the most majestic mountains weather with time. So, too, with Nan. It was a slow, gentle and mostly painless deterioration, more frustrating than anything because she was willing but increasingly unable to do the things she treasured, the chores that kept her productive and a "young 90."

Mowing the grass, then shoveling snow slipped from her grasp, as did her car keys and, with them, a large degree of freedom and independence. A flight of stairs. A long walk. Cooking. One by one, little by little, her world shrank and her shoulders stooped.

A trip to the hospital a year or two ago gave us the chance to have "that talk," not of birds and bees nor of cabbages and kings, but of life ... and death.

To her delight and, maybe, amazement, I leaned over her bedside, looked into her eyes and told her how much I treasured every moment of our years together.

Whenever the time came, I assured her I'd be fine. Any tears, I promised, would be in thanksgiving for her love and nurturing and for all we shared, chief among them the abiding faith in God's love and mercy that she passed on to me, and to which I cling today.

Her eyes twinkled. We both smiled.

The grave would be denied its victory and death would have no sting.

One of our special times was Brockway's annual community Thanksgiving Eve service at Lanes Mills church.

I'll be there this year, too, (7 p.m. Wednesday, if you're looking for something to do), thankful to be holding on to infinitely more than I let go of Sept. 17 when Nan's long and loving life came to a peaceful end.

The seat beside me may be empty this year. But I won't be alone.

Faith That Moves Mountains

Nan wasn't alone in her unshakable faith. It's easy to celebrate our faith when all is well. The true test comes when things aren't well and those times are where the rubber meets the road.

I was blessed to grow up in and later return to an old country church where faithful saints were on constant watch.

The family and friends of Marie Swanson gathered Wednesday at Beechtree Union Church outside Brockway to say their good-byes to a charming lady who blessed and enriched their lives, including mine.

Marie died peacefully Sunday at age 95.

Growing up, as we expand beyond our immediate family, people enter our lives and become "fixtures." So it was with Marie and her late husband, Yellie.

Over time, the layers of fixtures peel away, like an onion. And, as with an onion, each time a layer is peeled, there are tears. And there were Wednesday.

I grew up, church-wise, at Beechtree when I was 8, 9 and 10. The pastor then was George Felt. I returned 30 years later and a Felt was still pastoring, George's son Terry. Marie and Yellie were there, too, still fixtures.

Nick Hoffman

There were other ever-present personalities, notably Aldean "Dean" Lundblad; my Grandmother, the late Jo Hoffman, and the late Gladys Thompson.

They and Marie made a formidable quartet. Grandma lived to 90 and Gladys to 93. Dean turned 93 not long ago. Between them, they account for nearly four centuries of life, love and laughter.

Not that any of their lives were a bed of roses. Children of the Great Depression, they grew up hard. But, typical of the Greatest Generation, they endured. And the secret of their endurance was no secret at all: their abiding faith in God and his son, Jesus Christ.

An architect could explain the structural components at Beechtree, what makes it stand. But what holds it up - its pillars - is the faith of many, none more so than Marie, Gladys, Dean and Grandma.

We are taught that prayer moves the hand of God. That fearless foursome surely gave it a workout.

There were praying for me when I didn't know - or wouldn't acknowledge - that I needed prayer. Still they prayed, without ceasing. I know that in my case, the hand of God moved and still does.

I doubt they prayed for themselves, secure in the promise that God would provide for them. I imagine their prayers began by echoing St. Francis - "Oh Master grant that I may never seek ..." and ended with "Not my will, oh Lord, but Thine be done."

The four of them were in church for Sunday worship a few years ago; perhaps it was Mother's Day. All were in their regular seats.

The topic of the end of times had taken on decidedly more interest as world events cast a darkening pall across the earth.

War, famine, pestilence and death are represented by

He Was There All the Time

the Four Horsemen of the Apocalypse, the forces of evil that we are told will unleash their fury across the world before, as Christians believe, Christ returns to claim His kingdom in the ultimate battle between good and evil on the plains of Megiddo outside Jerusalem. Hence, Armageddon.

I thought about the Four Horsemen ... and our formidable Beechtree foursome. I pictured the vilest and most awful torments of hell, mounted and charging toward Marie, Gladys, Dean and Grandma.

The Horsemen wouldn't have a prayer ... but those four women surely would, as they always had. It wouldn't be a fair fight. I smiled.

I thought of that again Wednesday at Marie's funeral. I thought about fixtures and the passage of time. She was a comfort since my youth and the thought of her glowing smile and hearty chuckle comforts me still.

Not content with pointing the way, she walked it. Now, her journey is complete. Someday, mine will be, too.

But until then, my heart will go on singing, just as Marie's did.

A Piece Of Cake

In addition to having a lot of fun and making a lot of memories, Nan taught me so much that enables me to be "content," which I have often said is preferable to "happy." Contentment is deeper, more profound and if our faith is where it should be, more durable and lasting.

Contentment comes in many forms. One of them was when Nan was in the kitchen.

If Nan could only see me now ... she'd probably faint.

Nan - my late grandmother Jo Hoffman - and I had a wonderful life until her death at 90 two years ago.

Particularly special were the years we lived in the "old homestead" north of Brockway in a palatial 14-room Victorian masterpiece built by my great-great-great-grandfather, Redford Segers.

Within our abode, the living room was my domain, as it had been my grandfather Ken Hoffman Sr.'s, and the kitchen belonged to Nan, as well it should have.

She was to a kitchen what a maestro is to an orchestra. She was in her glory when her son and my father - "Duane" to her, one of his two middle names - was headed home from Omaha for a visit.

She sat at the table for hours shucking - or whatever one does to beans to begin the process of making from-scratch baked beans. Then came the scalloped potatoes and, finally, the piece de resistance, her meatloaf. Mmmmmmm ... yum.

As you might discern, there was little need for me to hone my limited cooking skills. Why? I ate like a king. And knew it. Why tamper with a good thing?

I envy guys who can cook. When I went to school, "home ec" was not held in the same regard as gym class and, not wanting to invite the wrath of my peers, I never ventured into that realm.

Oh, I can toss a pre-cooked entree into the microwave, warm a can of soup or scramble eggs but cooking and baking are, to be charitable, not my strong suit.

Since I moved into a house of my own five years ago, I've expanded my universe of cooking endeavors, which now include chili and beef stew. So far, so good, but I do make an annual donation to the DuBois and Sandy Township fire departments, just in case.

When I got home from work Saturday night, I flipped back and forth between two monster movies, the 1944 classic "House of Frankenstein" with Boris Karloff, Lon Chaney Jr. and John Carradine and the newly minted 2012 Big Ten Championship game between Wisconsin and Dr. Jekyll and Mr. Hyde, more commonly known as the Nebraska Cornhuskers.

In the Karloff flick, he's a twisted mad doctor bent on revenge who promises his assistant a new brain but decides the Monster (played by Glenn Strange, who went on to star as Sam the bartender on "Gunsmoke") needs one more. On the way to that operation, he digs up the Wolfman and promises him a brain, too.

I'm not a brain surgeon but my kitchen can double at times as a laboratory, and did so most recently Monday evening.

Nan liked to bake in the cold season, and blueberry

muffins were a staple. I had a hankerin' for some and, as luck would have it, I had a couple packs of blueberry muffin mix that hadn't reached their expiration date yet in the cupboard. Judging from the instructions, I could handle it.

I dumped a packet into a mixing bowl and added the milk. As I stirred, I realized I didn't have a muffin pan to put this gruel into ... and there didn't seem to be that much batter to begin with. Choosing to spare the remaining packet from loneliness, I dumped it into the bowl along with another half cup of milk.

Still no muffin pan but hey, what are a few muffins but a sliced up cake? Insert batter into cake pan - greased of course - and set timer to 15 minutes.

I've seen whopper muffins at Sheetz that surely didn't come out of a conventional muffin pan. So my muffin is 9 inches in diameter. As long as I don't eat it all at once - and as long as Nan didn't witness this sacrilege - I'll be OK.

A longtime family friend, JoAnn Keith, found Nan's gingersnap recipe and gave it to me last week.

Guess what I'll be doing between now and Christmas?

The Greatest Of These Is Love

During my stay at Valley Hope in Norton, Kan., we spent a lot of time studying "The Big Book," the bible of Alcoholics Anonymous.

One passage, found on page 164, has become a cornerstone of my approach to life. It reads:

"And acceptance is the answer to all my problems today. When I am disturbed, it is because I find some person, place, thing, or situation—some fact of my life — unacceptable to me, and I can find no serenity until I accept that person, place, thing, or situation as being exactly the way it is supposed to be at this moment. Nothing, absolutely nothing, happens in God's world by mistake. Until I could accept my alcoholism, I could not stay sober; unless I accept life completely on life's terms, I cannot be happy. I need to concentrate not so much on what needs to be changed in the world as on what needs to be changed in me and in my attitudes."

During my trips back to Norton, I tried to make a point to the patients.

If God put His arm around my shoulder and said, "Nick, you were dealt a lousy hand, and I want to make it up to you. I'm going to give you a mulligan. Pick an event that really hurt, and I'll change it."

I would humbly decline and explain, "God, if anything in my past were changed, everything else would be changed, too: People, places, things, memories. I wouldn't be who I am now. I'm satisfied and I'm content, because You've been with me all the way."

We were never promised that life would be free of sorrow and pain. What God does promise is that no matter what, He'll never leave us or forsake us. And God **never** breaks a promise.

A few years ago, a confluence of completely unrelated events over the course of one week showed how intricately interconnected our lives are. Maybe they weren't unrelated after all.

Rarely have our emotions been sent lurching on a roller coaster of agony and ecstasy like they have been in the last week.

Last Wednesday, the rains came in Elk County and before they stopped, Ridgway was crippled by a historic flood that few in the county seat have seen in their lifetimes.

As I tracked the flood story through the day, I prepared for Brockway's All-Sports banquet that night, where Francis "Bud" Grieneisen got his just desserts by being named Sportsman of the Year for his decades of dedication to Rover sports.

I share more of a connection with Bud than the portraits with "Photo by Grieneisen" as their tag in my archives. His No. 3 son, Dan, graduated with me and my Dad was best man when Bud married his high school sweetheart Jean Oct. 22, 1955, a date that, six years later, became my birthday.

I also shared a table that night with, among others, Steve Varischetti and, having not seen him in some time, he and I regaled each other with chatter and laughter, as we have since our days as students in the same, now expanded, cafeteria.

Little did we know how events that day would conspire to bring us together again a week later.

I made a trip to Ridgway Thursday evening, not to survey flood damage but to share the kindergarten graduation of my godson, Cameron Ceriani. In the blink of an eye, time has hurtled me from holding a newborn gingerly in my hands July 27, 2007, to sitting beside him in his kitchen while he reads to me, sounding out the words that he doesn't know and rarely having to ask me for help.

The Memorial Day weekend started Friday afternoon at DuBois Country Club in the Chamber of Commerce golf outing, shared with my boss, Devin Hamilton, classmate Paul Wilson, our photographer and IT guru, and Mark "Boogs" Becker, golf course superintendent at Owens Brockway Golf Course and another longtime compadre.

A day of relaxation Saturday turned into despair with news that a young woman from DuBois was killed in a canoe accident on the Clarion River at Portland Mills. The crest long gone, the swirling waters claimed a final casualty; Brittany Ann Baird was engaged to be married in September to Anthony "Jimmer" Varischetti, Steve's son.

The rest of the weekend was spent preparing for Monday's Memorial Day services. I was privileged to be the guest speaker at Falls Creek as it celebrated its lovely new Veterans Memorial Park then went to Morningside Cemetery in DuBois for that annual service, reminded at both venues of the love of country and allegiance to duty that led some to give all.

Tuesday brought another trip to Ridgway to chronicle the visit of Lt. Gov. Jim Cawley, state Sen. Joe Scarnati and state Rep. Matt Gabler. The cleanup continues, and will for a long time.

The day concluded at the Lakeview Lodge at Treasure Lake for DuBois Central Catholic's annual sports banquet. I shared the laughter evoked by Steelers defensive end Cameron Heyward with the Rev. Msgr. Charles Kaza, the school's interim president, who would early the next day don his vestments to preside at a funeral in Brockway.

And so Wednesday brought us full circle as 800 people filled the pews at St. Tobias for the funeral of Brittany Ann Baird. Eleven rows were occupied by her family and that of her fiance, Jimmer Varischetti.

The only thing in shorter supply than seats were dry eyes.

As Communion was served and the service neared its end, Msgr. Kaza nodded to Jimmer, who rose from his seat between his Dad and his Mom, Michele, and took to the lectern. His brother Angelo sat in a wheelchair in the aisle, having himself been injured in the canoe accident.

Then, the tear tap opened wide throughout the sanctuary.

With composure few men could summon, Jimmer told of the love-at-first-sight courtship that was to culminate at the altar at the end of September, days before what would have been Brittany's 26th birthday.

Then Jimmer lifted himself from unimaginable grief and said "I love you" one more time, defying death's sting and denying the grave its victory.

And after a week that flung thousands of people on journeys they wouldn't have chosen and couldn't have imagined, we were left with the nascent comfort, frail as it might be, that love can, and does, and will conquer all.

All In The Family

"Extended family" means a couple different things to me.

After they divorced, Dad and mom each married twice more. The net result is a family tree with a lot of branches.

Dad and his wife Fran have been married for 32 years. I call her Mom, because she has filled that role in every way (and is a great cook!). She calls me "the son she never had," and loves me as much as if I were. The three of us have a great relationship, one in which the miles apart have never mattered.

Dispensing with the "step-" and "half-" prefixes, I have three brothers and four sisters.

We're also "extended" in terms of distance between each other.

I see those who live in or near Omaha during my annual visits. The Masons - My sister Jenni is an elementary school teacher in Gretna, Neb. She and her husband Tom have four children: Sons Caden and Quinn, both enrolled at the University of Nebraska at Lincoln, and daughters Josie and Halle, still at home.

Patti Matney was Dad's second wife and is Jenni's mother. She has been a constant source of encouragement.

Sister Lisa is a hair stylist in Omaha. She has two

daughters - Emily, who is enrolled at the U.S. Military Academy at West Point, and Hannah, who is going to college in Arizona. Lisa and her husband Jason Mabey live in Omaha.

Brother Todd is an entrepreneur and businessman who lives in Jacksonville, Fla. Brother Brett is an obstetrician in Gainesville, Ga. Sister Audra is a teacher in Florida.

Sister Penny lives near Harrisburg, Pa. Brother Kevin lives in Brockway.

From top left to bottom right – Nick & Patti; Nick & the
Masons – Caden, Quinn, Josie & Halle; Nick w/Jason
& Lisa, Emily & Hannah; Graduation night 1979

Nick Hoffman

Jim and Heather, Alivia, Cameron and Savannah live in Smithville, Ohio. Jim's a big brother, the son I never had and my best friend rolled into one.

One big advantage for an old fuddy duddy like me in having so many young'uns to stay in touch with is having somewhere to turn to when technology overwhelms me, which is increasingly often.

My branch in the family tree will end when my life comes to an end. I'll leave no direct descendants. Once in a while, my mind will start playing "What if?" with me. What if I'd gotten married, had a family, etc., etc. There was a time when I found that unsettling. "What if" can be depressing if we invest too much time or thought to it.

I've learned that there's no use looking back. We have one life to live and have to go where the path leads. Dad shared his philosophy on that subject with me; "If you're going to have regrets, let them be for the things you did rather than those you didn't do." As usual, he's right.

I don't feel cheated. I wouldn't change anything even if I could because doing so would change everything else. If I did "this" instead of "that" I might not have turned left that Friday night and met Jim Ceriani. Instead, I might have gone home and gotten a phone call that made me rich, or I could have been killed in a head-on accident before I got home. I have to judge by results, by what I have and in that sense, I am content. Like Joe Walsh's tune from 1978 says, "Life's been good to me so far." The only change I'd make is to replace "Life's" with "God's."

From top left to bottom right Nick & Jim Ceriani;
Nick & Audra; Pa Segers; Dad & Nick w/Todd,
Jenni & Brett; Kevin, Penny & Nick; Nick & Mom (Fran)

Nick Hoffman

Epilogue

How do we come to that point where we decide whether to turn our lives over to the care of someone we cannot see, touch or carry on a two-way conversation with?

When was the last time you took a walk in the woods in autumn? Or looked into a night sky filled with twinkling stars? You saw Him.

How long has it been since a baby squeezed your finger as you smiled and made funny noises for him or her? You felt His touch.

Have you lain in bed, stared at the ceiling with tears streaming down your face and cried out, "Oh God," even though you haven't been formally introduced? He heard you.

Some of us have trouble "looking" for God; uncertain that He exists, not sure of what it is we're looking for and unsure if we're good enough to approach Him and ask for anything even if we do find Him.

He does ... and we're not. We can never be good enough. It is only through the mystery of "grace," - the unmerited favor of God – that we experience Him.

Each of us does eventually come to a fork in the road where the next step is up to us - to seek God, or not.

Those who know Him and accept His lordship over their lives, know the "peace that passeth all understanding" even in the most dire circumstances of their lives.

For those who have not found Him, there is hope. First,

there is still time, even though we don't know how much and the clock keeps ticking. Do not delay.

Second, the supply of God's love, mercy and grace is inexhaustible; I know because I've tried to exhaust it.

I believe in a God of second chances. He is a God of "more than" - more than we can imagine or hope for; more than we could ever do by and for ourselves, and certainly more than we deserve.

Even while we're wandering around aimlessly, bumping into things and making a general mess of our lives, He's arranging opportunities that will bring us to Him ... if and when we are ready and willing.

Maybe you are looking but haven't found Him. Or maybe you haven't started looking yet. That's OK. Take comfort in knowing that He's looking for you. He knows who you are and what you need. He's ready; are you?

Remember that every saint has a past ... and every sinner has a future.

This book could go on indefinitely. And it will. Inasmuch as you and I have "miles to go before we sleep;" we'll keep adding chapters. But this is where the pages end and we go our separate ways.

Life is full of twists and turns and potholes. And it's also full of good people who always seem to be at the right place at the right time with the right stuff.

My life bears witness to that. Yours does, too, and maybe you've thought about it. If you haven't, there's no time like right now to start.

Think of life as a relay race. Each of us runs our appointed "leg" and hands the baton off to the next runner when our turn is finished. The relay doesn't work if all the runners don't do their part.

The Apostle Paul made that point in Hebrews 12:1-2: "... let us lay aside every weight, and the sin which so easily ensnares *us,* and let us run with endurance the race that is set before us, looking unto Jesus, the author and finisher of *our* faith, ..."

While I was writing this book, I heard from a friend I'd lost touch with. He'd battled drug abuse and had spent time in jail. But he's found sobriety and is clinging to it. I encouraged him to "hang in there," and offered my shoulder to lean on if he needs to.

In reply he said, "You have always been good to me and I truly appreciate that. You are a good man and I have always looked up to you. Thank you Nick for being you."

We never know who's watching.

I mentioned the poem, "The Touch of the Master's Hand" earlier. It was written in 1921 by Myra Brooks Welch.

It says all that needs to be said and does so in a way that illustrates the difference God will make in our lives, if we let Him.

That difference can come from the most unexpected people at the most unexpected time or place in the most unexpected way. No matter who, when, where or how, He's there. In fact, He was there all the time.

This poem never fails to put a tear in my eye or a lump in my throat, and I think it is an appropriate ending for this book ... and for a new beginning for you and the road that lies ahead.

'Twas battered and scarred and the auctioneer
Thought it scarcely worth his while
To waste much time on the old violin,
But he held it up with a smile.

"What am I bid, good folks?" he cried.
"Who'll start the bidding for me?

"A dollar, a dollar; now two, only two
"Two dollars and who'll make it three?
"Three dollars once and three dollars twice ...
"And going for three, ..." But no.

From the room far back, a gray-haired man
Walked forward and picked up the bow
And wiping the dust from the old violin
And tightening up its strings,
He played a melody pure and sweet
As sweet as an angel sings.

The music ceased and the auctioneer
In a voice that was quiet, and low,
Said, "What am I bid for the old violin?"
And he held it up with the bow.

"A thousand dollars, now two, only two
"Two thousand and who'll make it three?
"Three thousand once and three thousand twice
"And going and Gone!" cried he.

The people cheered, but some of them cried,
"We do not quite understand.
"What changed its worth?
Quick came the reply: "The touch of the master's hand."

And many a man with life out of tune
And battered and scarred by sin
Is auctioned cheap to a thoughtless crowd
Much like the old violin.
A mess of pottage, a glass of wine,
A game and he travels on
He's going once, he's going twice;
He's going and almost gone.

But the Master comes, and the foolish crowd
Never can quite understand
The worth of a soul, and the change that's wrought
By the touch of the Master's hand.

Top left to bottom right – new sportswriter; Graduation speaker; On my swing; Following through on the Great Plains; Nick & Congressman Murtha

Printed in the United States
By Bookmasters